ANCIENT SECRETS FOR
Modern Day Success

Rediscovering The Wisdom That Leads
To Health, Wealth and Happiness

Jared W. Jones

Ancient Secrets For Modern Day Success

By: Jared W. Jones

Copyright © 2012 Jared W. Jones. All rights reserved.

Printed in the United States of America

978-0-9849585-0-4

Legal Disclaimer

Dedicated

To

My Beautiful Wife, Carrie &
My Amazing Sons, Bryce, Connor & Talon
For your constant love & support.
Thank you for standing by me.

And to

My Wonderful Parents: Roger & Linda
For being truly inspiring Christians and
always being there for me.

CONTENTS

INTRODUCTION

> *We do not choose to be born. We do not choose our parents. We do not choose our historical epoch, the country of our birth, or the immediate circumstances of our upbringing. We do not, most of us, choose to die; nor do we choose the time and conditions of our death. But within this realm of choicelessness, we do choose how we live.*
>
> **Anonymous**

When you combine faith in God, belief in yourself and lessons from times past, the result is often staggering – a life filled with purpose, fulfillment and happiness. At birth, each of us is set upon a path, but not alone. We are given a map, a blueprint to live by – a secret tome of knowledge that often lies dormant as a result of circumstance, hopelessness and fear. For most lost in the world, life becomes a daily struggle. But it was never meant to be viewed in darkness. This book is about unlocking the potential you were born with, and relearning the ancient lessons that will lead you back to your destined path. This is why I urge you to read this book with care.

#1: Retaining Ancient Wisdom

Read this book with a ruler, and underline (or highlight, if reading on an electronic device) phrases that resonate with you. Don't underline/highlight in haste, or the revisiting of these truths will distract - and possibly even repel you - from coming back to these points.

Anything that affects you, can affect change in your life. Examine the wisdom and laws here that influence you, and review them regularly, so that you don't lose focus, and are able to overcome any obstacle placed in your path.

#2: Taking Notes

I'd encourage you to write notes on these pages. I write things like *"Act on this, key, develop my own plan from this section, train my children, or my team from this particular point"*.

#3: Revisiting Inspiration

Revisit the key points in this book at least once a month. I revisit the truths in this book on a daily basis, or if I'm really busy, at least once per week. I also believe that Pareto's 80/20 principle applies to this book - which means that 20% of the book is meat, heavy, and good for you to digest, while the other 80% while valuable, doesn't have the same power level of content of the original 20%. This isn't the same for everyone, so as point #1 suggests, be vigilant when reading this book, to extract the ideas and illustrations that affect you.

#4: Your Plan of Action

Outside of this book, write an action plan. Summarize your ideas, and make sure that they are not lost once you put the book down. The inspiration that you take from these pages, may be an opportunity that won't spark in your mind for several years, if ever again. Writing them down, is the first step to training your mind to own these ideas – then add faith, and the perseverance to bring about the physical manifestation of your new desires. All of which result from reading this powerful book.

My Story

I grew up in very humble beginnings, in a small town South of Orlando - Saint Cloud Florida. My mom was a private school teacher who earned extremely low wages, and often even less than minimum wage. She would work long, thankless hours, and I believe it was because she felt it was her ministry, her way of serving the world. Sure, she had a college degree in education, and had even taught in public schools, but felt her calling was to help a private school with limited resources, offer children a quality education. My dad was one of the early 'cast members' at Disney World, and was a horticulturist there.

My dad wore a lot of hats, as I remember, which could be the key reason why I try to wear so many myself. I remember growing up and watching my dad preach. There were times when he pastored churches (mostly when I was very young). My dad was an impressive preacher, at least to me, and I remember the honor that people afforded him and me, for being his son.

He often worked side jobs, or ran his own small business, and I was always his 'labor', and proud to be so. Dad pulled me out of bed early for countless Saturday mornings, for a couple of bucks an hour and a cheeseburger! Eating out in my home was a huge deal, so I gladly went along and spent hours outside digging ditches in the Florida sun, cutting through massive oak tree roots.

Like many families in our area, mine worked extremely hard, and did not have much to show for it. I don't recall having new clothes, ever, until sixth or seventh grade. My first pair of Nike's when I was 13 or 14 was a "thirty Dollar" pair of shoes, a very big deal to me back then.

My family's hard work was dosed out week after week in incredible quantity, but it never seemed to have any real return. My extended family, are great people. My aunts and uncles, and grandparents gave us great Christmases and Birthdays, even though at the time, I didn't realize that they were the normal middle to upper middle class people, I thought they were RICH!

Back To Childhood

We had an interesting mix of transient cars. There was the Ford Fairmont with the crazy wood panels. A myriad of Datsun's and vinyl seats. Those vinyl seats were mean, when you know that all of these cars had no air conditioning, and Florida is quite hot and humid nearly the entire year. Riding in a car with AC was the coolest thing. I remember when riding in a friend's car with air conditioning, at the time, felt to us(my brother and me) like we were riding in a limousine!

Our home was very rough – we had a single, wide mobile home with some odd structure built over it to add additional rooms, on a slab foundation. But, there was tons of land to run and play on, five acres of it. We grew up running around, and riding bikes for miles, and just having a good time. The ponds on our property had fish. My neighbors had acreage as well, and they had even more ponds, and even more fish.

If we got sick of fishing, we went exploring in the bush. It's amazing we were never bitten by Rattlesnakes or Water

Moccasins, even though we stepped on a few. Man, what a time! We would get out early, and come in late. We rode bikes and go-carts forever.

As I got older, I discovered a new hobby that would seize my attention. Remarkably, at a time when most kids were getting heavy into high school sports, or girlfriends, or various extracurricular activities - I began a love affair with work.

Organized labor for me was the most amazing thing. To be able to earn a check, and go out and acquire things was indescribable. I remember the silliest things being so exciting, going out to get my own hair cut, and when I wanted to, getting clothes (which I was and still am frugal about to this day), and of course, going out to eat! Work itself impressed me. I was obsessed with pay raises! I really looked over the system that I worked under and worked out all of the details.

I worked extremely hard and loved every second of it. I was always paid at the highest portion of the grades given; when I could not get another raise, I often worked 30 to 40 hours, even while going to high school. When I got out of high school, I was quickly promoted into management and developed as a leader at 18 and 19 years of age. I was very immature and admittedly, it was very trusting of my superiors to place 20 to 30 people in my care at that time - I must have been a pain to work with.

In the retail industry, I was a 'clean-up' manager. I would be sent to a store that had a huge glut of ordered inventory that wasn't making its way out of the front of the store. I would be brought in, turn over staff, and work tirelessly to get the store's inventory load at a manageable level. That position took years off, of my life. When I arrived, I'd instantly be met with pushback as to why I wanted to 'rehire' a number of people who were already there, and often times, the up-line wouldn't let me do it.

If an employee didn't care enough to give you 8 hours work then they generally would steal from you in other ways. So, I knew if I 'managed' those types close enough, then they would work themselves out of the organization. That is exactly what would happen. In 3 months, I would have hired an entirely new team, and in 8 to 12 months, hundreds of thousands of dollars in previously parked inventory would be out and sold. I worked ridiculous hours to pull this off, and overworking has its consequences.

I remember my girlfriend then (now wife) was riding with me in her car, and I fell asleep at the wheel. I spun the car completely around, going 70 miles an hour and we are fortunate that we did not die that night.

When I was around 19 years old, Carrie joined the Air Force and when she did, she was eventually moved to Las Vegas to be stationed as a Labor and Delivery technician. But before she did, I met her in Texas at her Tech School, and Married her in Wichita Falls Texas.

Wichita Falls was our honeymoon residence for a month after we got married, and before we moved to Vegas. This place was the first that we remember, truly being on our own. We lived on peanuts. I worried often, obsessively thinking, 'we have 4 days to get by on $24 for groceries.' Kool-Aid was a premium beverage, and pasta was our normal fare. Carrie and I stayed in a musty old apartment complex that rented for around $350 a month. It was far from nice, but that short month flew by and it was time to go to Vegas, where our lives would change forever.

The Changing Times

When we got to Vegas, the military took Carrie to the Base Hospital where she assisted in delivering babies for the next 3 years or so. The retail company that I worked for since being in high school, transferred me for a short while in Texas - but didn't have any branches this far in the west, so I had to quit. When I got to Vegas, I applied for similar jobs like the one I had given up, and all of the comparable companies said I had to start at the entry level, to work in their organizations. That caught me by surprise. I felt sure that my credentials would turn heads and help them see something in me. Surely, they would fast track me because of my experience?

I was horribly wrong. So, I took the next logical step and I applied to the companies that sell to those stores. I was hired by a Fortune 500 company and worldwide brand, and worked my way into their top grossing position for my sales level. With this success followed a pay increase.

I loved it, and with that, we were able to buy our first home in 2001. At the same time, my second love affair would begin – *Real Estate*. I remember soon after I closed on our home, that I bought 'Rich Dad, Poor Dad's Guide to Investing,' and was completely blown away by the concept of buying a home - and having someone else pay it for you! All that cash flow! I was a big thinker, and wanted to take that process and do it over and over again.

A guy named Daryll became one of my best friends at the company, and reached out to me. He said he had bought a home as well, and that the professional that sold it to him was sharp, hard working like we were, and a WHOLE lot wealthier for his toil. With that, we felt that real estate school was where we needed to be.

Within 3 months of getting my license, I decided to go full time. Then the doubts came. I was lying in bed, saying, "What are you thinking Jones! You don't have a regular paying job, and you have bills!" Being self-employed looked a lot better to me before I quit my job. Now it was go-time. Within months of getting my license, my wife and I, had just bought our second home, and decided to rent out the first one. That was not so bad, but our first home was $120,000, and the new mortgage on our second home was $275,000! It made for a few more nights of staring up at the ceiling contemplating - but the months that followed, were good to us. By mid 2003, I was busy getting my feet wet in the soaring Vegas market.

The Property Boom

By late 2003, early 2004 – I worked in one of the craziest markets ever, and it is likely something I will never see again. Homes would go on the market and be sold before the sign hit the front yard!

Multiple offers on homes, 15 or 20 offers deep, were not uncommon. A certain builder in town would raise prices every couple of weeks, by $15 or 20k, and all other builders would follow suit! It was incredible. Homebuyers would have to come in with insane amounts to get a contract, and any hoop a buyer could be forced to jump through, would be thrown out there. The market shot up like a rocket, and did not really back off until 2005.

During 2005 to 07, I felt like a fish out of water. It was almost surreal to see the market coming down in value. All of the sales data that had been kept on real estate for the last 40 or so years, had always shown a steady incline. The buzzwords in the media for real estate is that, "It's never really gone down" historically speaking. Sure, there were pockets of depreciation here and there, but seeing it happen was really strange. As a result of the falling prices, buyers and sellers alike didn't know what to do with the market, and sales dropped.

These years were very stressful for me; I had to buy the real estate company out from a dear friend and business partner due to overlapping focus, our interests going in separate directions. I had around 30 independent agents as well, that had to be afforded month after month, so to make ends meet, I racked up huge credit debts.

The Changing Tides

Nothing lasts forever. Late 2003 into 2004, not only brought an amazing turn of events in the market, but age 25 would deal me a blow, that I wasn't ready for. My dad had developed cancer around 2002, was operated on and treated - and reported a clean bill of health. My dad and I got along real well. As I have indicated, much of my work ethic comes from dad, and we were kindred spirits. We spoke more than any family member I have now, or have had since.

Every couple of days, we would talk about what was going on in my life, and knowing that my dad came from very little, deep down inside, I wanted to go out and crush it in life to make him proud. In my early 20s, I felt that course taking shape. But life doesn't always go as planned.

Late 2003, on one of our frequent calls, he reported the cancer's return. I don't recall many Christmases (by year) but I remember 2003 vividly.

I landed in Florida, and on the way into my hometown, I stopped to see my mom to surprise her at her classroom, where she taught at the time. Mom cautioned me, "Your dad is really eager to see you, but he is not looking well". We left the school to go to my wife's childhood home to see her father, and my dad drove up (which was odd), but you got the sense that this morning, he felt the urgency to see me. You have to understand dad. He was a tree trunk of a man. He wasn't really tall, but he had a wide neck, big muscular arms, and huge legs. He was a big strong guy.

As I saw him get out of the car, after not seeing him for several months, I really wasn't ready for what I was about to see. He had gone from a 200 plus pound guy, to right around 100 pounds, and he was so frail at 48 years old - beyond anything I could have ever imagined. When you see someone in this scenario, your first instinct is to really avoid the obvious, to not let them visually believe that their change is so evident and affecting you.

He ran up to me and hugged my neck and I could not help but break down and cry. I tried to hold it back, but was overwhelmed. It broke my heart to have to believe that my father's mortality was now in jeopardy. It was not too long after that, that I had to bury my dad in Florida. It was one of the hardest events of my young life. I have a tape of the last sermon I heard dad preach, and it thrills my soul to hear a man who was extremely sick, surrounded by a crowd of people – saying "Be your best, no matter if you are on 'life's mountain top" or in an eventual valley". I cherish that.

My oldest son who was the only one of my 3 boys to meet dad, still called him "Skinny Pe-Pa", as that is his earliest recollection of this mass of a man broken down by cancer. When cancer hits close to home, you have a disdain for such a horrible disease, that few can match. My Pastor, Dr. David Teis here in Vegas says, that he prays for those in our church who are battling cancer, every single day. Remember those people in prayer. They need them.

This book will help you realize your true purpose, as you reach deep inside yourself, to tap an inner strength that has been lying dormant all of this time.

Life is full of ups and downs – but they are no excuse not to live life to your fullest potential. In these pages, you are going to find ancient wisdom, inspired by my life's journey, and timeless knowledge I have accumulated along the way. I believe it will bring you success, happiness and peace across all facets of your life.

CHAPTER ONE

THE WISDOM OF FOCUS

> *One reason so few of us achieve what we truly want, is that we never direct our focus; we never concentrate our power. Most people dabble their way through life, never deciding to master anything in particular.*
> **– Tony Robbins**

Overcoming Tragedy, Embracing Challenges

I believe in any horrible event, God is working through our lives – he has a motive in that hardship, beyond what you can see. There are always people that you can care for, share to, and comfort, and only you will be given that gift at that time. God focused my dad on what was most important when life's moments for him were so precious. I did not know until his funeral, but dad had shared the light of Christ to the nurses, the oncology staff, and folks he came in contact with.

The preacher at the funeral held up a list of over 40 people who were converted to Christianity as a result of dad's testimony. As selfishly as I wanted dad back, there are 40 people whose eternal destinies are forever changed, because dad gave at a time when it could be so easy to focus on himself. It is a lesson we should all be reminded of from time to time.

Dad raised the bar for me, and I am convinced every time I tell this story, that I am healthy and there are so many people that I need to reach. For that reason, this book is dedicated to *Roger Jones*. I miss you dad. As I told him on his bed before I left him in Florida - knowing I would never see him again here on this earth, "I will see you again, whether it's here or not."

Loss is the deepest, most desperate pain we can feel. It touches a part of your soul so powerful, it threatens to destroy the person you are, and all you have done in the world. That's why when your soul is in mourning, you realize the weight of your deeds. More often than not, they amount to nothing.

Life's Little Distractions

In life, we are never present, and we never really live. If you are in sales, or in any profession, when you are at work – you're thinking about the kids, the dog, and being on the couch at home. When you're at home, you'll find yourself thinking about what you didn't do at work, some plan that you need to execute, or some prospect that you need to close.

You can compare it to the lull you feel when watching television. As a spectator, the days roll by, but your mind is never fully present. That is why so many people feel disconnected, and desperate to regain some sense of reality. More often than not, reality at that point, is too painful to bear, and too far gone to salvage.

Suddenly you look around, and nothing feels familiar. How did your life end up here? When did this happen? How did you let it get this bad?

There are days of your life that you have lived, but have never truly experienced. Steve Jobs (of Apple fame) almost to an extreme - contemplated the morbidity of life to 'focus' himself on the moment. We often never even come to this place until we are faced with someone's passing, or are at a funeral to celebrate a life not with us any longer. I believe there is balance here as with anything in life.

Some of us live life as if we are strapped into a roller coaster ride. There are fleeting moments of build up anticipation and excitement – but then it rushes by so fast that you don't really have your bearing on where you are, at any given time. Always take time frequently in life to challenge yourself. What really matters? Not to the world, but to you as individual.

Start with your spiritual health and well-being. Most of us let these crucial parts of ourselves decay. Yet our spirit is where our strength lies. Our faith is where the magic happens. Our soul is the defining part of us, the essence that needs to be filled. When we ignore our spiritual wellbeing, we veer off God's chosen path for us. Fulfillment and happiness begins and ends in the spirit.

Are you where you're supposed to be in life? Are you humble, giving, and purpose driven? Are you clear on your purpose to mankind, spiritually speaking? If you are not, may I recommend a personal retreat? Take a planned half day alone to go somewhere on your own, and take inventory of yourself to see what you should be giving.

Go to a park, a lake (or body of water), a tranquil hike, or go somewhere alone, with a pad of paper.

Start by taking 15 minutes and clearing your mind of everything. If you want to bring a Bible to read to start off this day, do so. We all should be in service in our lives, it doesn't matter who you are or how busy you think you are, you must be teaching, sharing, or giving to someone else. If you aren't nurturing your spirit like this, you're not living up to your God given purpose. The more self-concerned you become, the more depressed and unfulfilled you will be in life.

BHAGS: Big Hairy Audacious Goals

Up into the 3rd or 4th quarter of 2007, since the time I got my license, I had always done normal conventional real estate transactions. But, the availability of those deals in a falling market was horribly narrow. As a result of the normally fast paced, high volume real estate that I was used to, I had high cost, and low revenues, that literally nearly bankrupted me that year.

My attorney did in fact look everything over, and tell me to start planning for a bankruptcy to occur. There is something amazingly relieving when you have been fighting a massive debt battle and keeping on 30 agents plus 4,000 square foot of commercial space, and then to take council from someone who says "You don't have enough to keep going, let it go" – and you sit back and go hmmm, I hadn't thought of that!

It's a bittersweet pill. That year though, God opened the door to something that would change my life, the foreclosure industry had arrived. Late that year, an asset manager from one of the mortgage companies called me, and started working a deal. It was direct which is highly unusual – most of the time, they have an agent that works for them, that they call, and then that agent calls you, but it's never direct.

I was able to put that transaction through swiftly, and the mortgage rep said, "Why aren't you working with us?" I replied, "Because you never asked me!" That event started a new strategic plan for me and the company. The strategic plan was this: continue on serving the conventional market well, but to add to that a department that could manage the needs of the default industry (in pre-and post foreclosure).

That move alone, was so brilliant, that I cannot discount the hand of divine intervention on it, at least in terms of me personally. I lightened the load at Horizon. I took all 30 of the agents that worked with me and 'walked them over' - essentially giving the assets of the business to another local company, so that I could lower cost, lower attention on brokerage related issues, and get down to the business of executing this strategic plan.

Costs, with the 'walkover' were also lowered. Horizon would become a one-room office of around 12x10 feet, but with growth of the business, we wouldn't be there long. With just me and the company's corporate broker (who by the way believed in me enough to stick around, even though it was now ONLY me and her, the other 30 agents were gone – most would have left in such an arrangement.)

The Business 360

As time went on, the execution of the new business plan went well. Costs were low, and cash started to flow. I needed a sidekick. One of my best friends (I don't advocate you working with friends unless they have the right attitude), Curtis, was one of the 30 agents.

They say, that 'tomorrow' is the world's greatest labor saving device in existence, and I believe that with him. He is sharp, and much of the direction I have taken in the business has been with summonsing his council on things, but he doesn't move on things quickly. When I downsized the company in 2007, I walked all of the agents over, including MYSELF, the owner, and there was no one remaining... except Curtis! We kid with each other now,

years later, that everyone left and Curtis was the only captain on the ship.

So, I took Curtis on, and then eventually a second hire and the three of us were too cramped in the accommodations we had, and soon decided to move out of the little 120 square foot office. We then went up to 800 square feet. We kept executing, and cash flow was moving, and business was getting better and better with God's blessing. In fact, I had gone from the brink of bankruptcy, to now seeing some of the best years ever. During this time, not only did I professionally downsize, but I did on the personal side as well.

Understand that from 2002 to 2007, my wife and my businesses were incredibly successful. We drove all of the expensive cars and always had big houses, both with big monthly mortgage and car payment statements hitting the mailbox every month.

I had the new BMW, or the Hummer truck, or the Escalade with rims, you name it, I probably drove it. We had big homes in some of the most prestigious Las Vegas neighborhoods while still in my mid 20's.

I had housing costs alone that were 6 figures in total per year, and no one really came up along side of me and said 'you dummy,' - because that's exactly what I was. I grew up in humble beginnings and never knew what to do with it. In hindsight, it really is not much better to have money that comes in - and goes straight out to payments, than to have no money at all.

Ancient wisdom says that owing someone, is basically putting yourself in slavery. It also says, that if you cannot pay, then you are likely to have your very bed snatched out from underneath you, which is exactly what we see when our country goes into depression. It's not only our beds getting snatched, but our nice heated leather Lexus car seats.

I learned that for 'Modern Day' success, you can't measure what you can afford by how many monthly payments you believe you can make. You measure affordability on whether or not you can buy the thing with cash, without raiding your emergency savings, and walk out the store with the item.

Debt and Downscaling

At this time, I could not avoid personal downsizing and boy what an incredible shock it was. We sold our homes, and went to live in a nice rental property that was one third of the cost of the mortgage we were used to paying. The irony here was that I was selling 10 homes a month or so, and not owning a home myself at the time. We got rid of the expensive cars and bought the best, "classic" (also known as used) cars that we could with the money we had saved.

I went from driving my nice black big body BMW to driving a nine-year-old pink Cadillac. I used to tell people that it's a preacher's car. When I talk to agents, I let them know that when you drive an old car, yet are still smart about the business, that people might buy from you, just because they feel sorry for you! I thought, hey, with this car, if real estate doesn't work out, I can start dealing drugs, and this car could work perfectly for that! I had to look on the bright side.

I almost became superstitious about that old musty car, because since the day I started driving it, the business and cash flow consistently improved from there. In truth, it had nothing to do with the car, but the fact that we had downsized everything, and there was capital to work our venture with, to multiply it and make it grow. That is one thing people miss when they stretch themselves to the max with car payments, credit cards and housing payments - is that Americans at their core, are entrepreneurs.

We create, we contribute, and we bless the world with our ideas, and when we strap ourselves so thin – we take our 'opportunity' capital away, and the thing that we know we could do.

For example, create a shirt company that does something cool, or to launch a revolutionary tool - and it never happens. Those gifts that could be given out in mass, never go, because we can't do it. Credit has an opportunity cost that many American's never see. Debt limits your personal potential. It strangles every major opportunity that comes along in your life.

You may think you are enjoying the fruits of your labor, but all you are doing is strapping yourself down, to an inescapable lifestyle of struggle, stress and stagnation.

Over time, the office became cramped, and we expanded up from the 800 square feet. About 18 to 24 months later, the office literally had 2 to 4 people working in every room. I remember just before we moved out, that I was standing in the middle of the office greeting my CPA, who wanted to meet with me. We looked around, and could not find a seat to sit in!

I believed now, in not paying a lease for anything that I wasn't using, and this was definitely using that space. I had to meet my CPA that year, in my car outside the office. We moved into a larger headquarters, and were now in the biggest offices we had seen, since the company started. We now command nearly 10,000 square feet, in three different sites in Las Vegas, and Henderson. As I write this, we are executing plans to move into two other states in the region, as well as Nevada's northern market.

The company I owned, where I once walked over the only 30 agents I had, now has over 100 agents and closes in the neighborhood of a billion dollars in real estate in the Vegas Valley per year.

My story is one of a dumb kid, with blessings and God given talents, getting into an industry at 22, and doing it wrong for several years, burning through hundreds of thousands of dollars, and revising the plan, and doing it again, but differently.

Learning From Past Mistakes

The first approach was the modern day pop culture approach – the thing you hear about in the media, the credit card riches that don't last. The second approach was built on principles that you will read in this book, on Ancient wisdom and God given immutable laws. Your life may not be what you want it to be right now, but it can be. If you are walking a pop culture path, you will need an intervention. But I assure you, you can have all that you want out of life, if you follow the Ancient Wisdom in this book.

I love real estate. I like the *business* of real estate, I like real estate as an investment vehicle, I enjoy helping buyers and sellers get what they want when the market is good, and I find no toil in having to roll up my sleeves, and work to clean up the real estate market, when the Las Vegas market has tanked. Often, my personal investments surround real estate, because this is what I know best.

A good friend of mine and I, love to stir one another up. We both have consistently ranked at the top of the field, in both Nevada and in the Nation in real estate volume. We go at it fiercely. We are both ultra-competitive. We are constantly pushing each other to get up earlier, to do one more rep, to break another sales record, and we feed off this regularly.

Iron Sharpens Iron

Ancient wisdom says that iron sharpens iron. Air doesn't sharpen iron, and a sponge won't do it either. If you do not have a strong positive influence in your life, you are missing out.

You need iron on iron. The friction serves both pieces of iron, it is mutually beneficial. The truth is, you are not going to be your best without the challenge and accountability of a good friend. I want to state further, that while a spouse can be challenging and supportive, this isn't ideally who the compelling 'iron' friend should be. I believe this to be true, because they are inside of your world. They live with you.

We are trained to temper our 'truth' with our spouses, not force it out. "Honey do I look fat in this dress?" Of course not! "Honey, do you think I am still a handsome dude?" - Yes honey, why do you ask? What's the difference? Your friend has an outside interest, they don't care if you go to bed flustered because you were honest, they will tell it to you straight. This brings me to the BHAG principle.

My friend and I set BHAGs for each other. Big Hairy Audacious Goals.

First, we pick a goal, and then we make it huge. I mean stretch it to the max, and then add hair! The way this is done, is if you think you can sell 30 widgets next year, you make a plan to sell 40 widgets instead. Then you add hair. Adding hair means you compress the time limit of delivering that goal as well" Now, under the example that you will sell those 40 widgets, if you would logically take one year to do that, you would cut that timeline down to 10 months.

Now, you're going to sell those 40 widgets in only 10 months! My 'iron' accomplice and I do this at will, and we are relentless. He and I both take on these challenges. It does not matter if we're in an obvious position to win the challenge, we still launch ourselves at it with gusto.

It's really a great exercise. I have honestly learned more about myself and my creativity, by taking on some insane goal, and then pushing my creative imagination to the limit. BHAG's will force you to think things that you have never had to think before. It will stretch your mind in new directions. Imagine setting a goal so crazy, that you have to actually sit down, with every ounce of juice and say to yourself, "How am I going to gain access to $10,000 in the next month" Or, "What do I have to give, to get in return, $200,000 in the next quarter?"

What about having such an insane BHAG, that you would have to sit down and say "Who do I have to be, to gain $1 million in the next 2 or 3 months!" and then work it backwards. Do it right now. Think of a specific goal that is so outrageous that you can't see the end of it. Do you have friends in your life that would ask that of you? Take stock in your acquaintances – are they 'iron' friends or 'sponge' friends? What about your goals? Do you have a BHAG or is it just a BAG!

Lessons in Friendship

The marines are some of the most talented and fit people in the Armed Forces. I have a friend, Mark, who left after high school and went to boot camp, and busted his butt for several weeks. When I saw my friend later, he didn't even look like the same guy, and his attitude was very different.

He used to be tacky and unfocused, a constant clown. When he came back, you could tell that he had a sense of pride and maturity that I had never seen in him before.

He said, "Jared, I don't know what it is, but I have this new bright future, and I have changed so much – but my friends haven't really gone anywhere", and oddly, "I really don't have anything to say to them anymore." Mark went on for hours, and what I took from the situation, was that Mark had hung around 'sponge' friends, and had experienced low-level influence for a long time.

When he joined the military, he had enjoyed a new experience. He had interacted with 'iron' influences. The bar was raised so high in him mentally and physically, that he literally 'outgrew' his former base of acquaintances back home, and that was alright.

Have you ever heard the saying, "Rich people only have rich friends?" From an outside perspective, this may seem to have class-based motives.

You can only be friends with someone, if they earn the same as you do. Traditionally it's easy to think that this is because they go to better places, and spend more money. But, that's not the reason at all.

Successful people tend to be 'iron' influences. They thrive off challenges, highly competitive markets and equally as driven friendship circles. Moreover, they correctly reject the influence of sponge friends.

God tells us to love everyone, despite their status or motives. But this doesn't mean that you should litter your life with poor friendship decisions.

Even one iron friend can catapult you into another league. Do they inspire you, push you, force you to be better, work harder and tap into creative thoughts you never would have had without them? These are your iron friends. Keep them close. Always remember that iron sharpens iron.

The Little Give and Take

A little extra sleep, a little more slumber, a little folding of the hands to rest, then poverty will pounce on you like a bandit, scarcity will attack you like an armed robber.
- PROVERBS 6:10-11

The worst thing that we see in hard times is the inevitable downward spiral of life. There are times when what you have been doing does not work anymore - or the inevitable law of diminished returns takes over. What you have been doing just does not work as well. The vicious cycle starts, efforts yield less, then negativity sets in, and then the deep-set terror found in hopelessness.

I have seen more millionaires lose out because they didn't stay vigilant on this particular bit of ancient wisdom, than I'd like. They go to the stable, and take out the horse - this means that they find a venture or service that they could use to provide for themselves - then the horse takes off, and business is good.

Inevitably, something changes and the market isn't there for that service, in quite the same way, and the horse starts to limp. The problem is, that the rider is still on and kicking the heck out of that horse. Harder and harder they kick, and pretty soon they're sitting on the horse, and that horse should be in the ICU. The rider should have switched horses all along.

Vigilance is a major key to long-term performance. It goes hand in hand with focus. Ancient wisdom calls for us to never 'fold our hands' not even a 'little.' In this proverb, 'a little' is key to everything. This term 'little' is so true in the game of life.

One day you wake up and notice you're 30 pounds overweight. But you didn't get that way by eating big one weekend. It was just one more bite, one extra helping – the collection of little things that does us in!

That 'little' more than we should eat, day after day, and we are cooked. Conversely, that person, that gives a little more time, that pays a little more attention to the numbers, that uses 'little' in a positive way – well, the overall impact isn't a little - it's a measurable distance that this person puts against the competitor.

We are very fearful of the price that a little more effort will render at times. "If I give a little more, the sacrifice is just immense." The sacrifice is not immense when compared to the person who is wanting, the person who is scraping by, or the person who ends life looking back on a vision that failed, because they stopped a 'little' short at every milestone.

We aren't fearful of the price, we want the price. The price pays us back multitudes more than what it really cost us. Getting out of bed just a little earlier, and getting a hard long day in and being home to spend those precious moments with your family, isn't a price paid, it's a gift. It's a weekend that rewards you with deserved rest, and with a family that appreciates the sacrifice. You don't hate the price, you appreciate the price. Ancient wisdom says you win or lose, by the 'little' inches in life.

The Amplification of Focus

There are a lot of great lessons to be learned in this chapter, on how to regain focus, and promote it in our lives.

Here is a refresher on the most crucial points, and a section you should revisit whenever you are feeling unfocused, bogged down by that passive, spectator mindset.

- Concentrate the power of focus in your life, to hone in on what you would like to change. Then change it!

- God works in your life by blessing you with little miracles, opportunities and challenges. Each has a purpose, and it is up to you to discern this purpose.

- Stay present in your life by living in the moment. Happiness materializes from moments when your mind is focused on the mundane and the exceptional. Experience life by clinging to these present moments. When your mind is unfocussed, it allows life and happiness to pass you by.

- Death helps us remember the truly important things in life. Try to hold on to this mentality, so that you remember your purpose, and why nurturing your spirit is the most crucial part of your existence.

- Be humble and giving, always – to stay focused on your purpose. Indulging the modern pop culture mantra of self-importance will only lead to depression, failure and hopelessness.

- Stop regularly to take stock of your life and its direction. A future goal may lie up ahead, but what about your focus right now? Does your life hold purpose and meaning right now? If you need to, take a break to reassess this goal.

- Set BHAG's for yourself. Big Hairy Audacious Goals serve to push you harder, so that you reach an untold potential inside yourself. Begin with what you can do. Then increase it. Then add hair! These insurmountable goals are that much sweeter when you achieve them. You have no limits!

- When your mind is always in focus, you are able to spot opportunities that could change your life. Never be complacent about change. It will happen with or without you. A focused mind adapts, and forges a new path to success. Adaptability is the right hand of a focused mind.

- Owing someone money, is the greatest form of slavery. Not only physical slavery, but mental too – as your potential and ability to be successful is greatly stunted by financial burden. Debt has no place in the life of a focused person.

- Ego and modern entrapments will try to hold you back, and keep you down. Our debt driven society is made up of people living 'spectator' lives. Instant gratification is a myth. Put these aside and downscale, so that you can reinvest your focus in potential, creativity and innovation.

- Iron sharpens iron. Right now, you may have many sponge friends. But you need a strong positive influence in your life to push you further. Find a friend that lives in your space, that can help you achieve greatness, and BHAGs. A sponge can't sharpen iron. Choose your friends wisely.

- Becoming an iron influence may mean that you have to set along a different path, than your older sponge friends. As you grow, many will be left behind. But this is a positive step, and core to your daily focus.

- A little goes a long way. In your life, you will be faced with more 'little' challenges than large ones. Being focused means having the presence of mind to make the right micro-decisions, which will add up to large success over time. Never forget the little give and take.

The wisdom of focus is the *first step* you need to take along your new path to health, wealth and happiness. Keep these lessons handy, and re-read them whenever you can. Being focused will help you take action when it's necessary. That also means refocusing on the lessons in this chapter when you need to.

CHAPTER TWO

THE WISDOM OF DESIRE

> *A person should set his goals as early as he can and devote all his energy and talent to getting there. With enough effort, he may achieve it. Or he may find something that is even more rewarding. But in the end, no matter what the outcome, he will know he has been alive.*
>
> **– Walt Disney**

Desires of The Heart, Mind and Body

You've heard people say, if you want it bad enough, you can make it happen. At the very heart of all achievement lies desire. It creates passion, channels focus and manifests in swift action. But desire in today's world has become something unattainable. People are quick to desire, and that is as far as it goes. The bridge between desire, goals and achievements has been broken.

Strong desire coupled with a success driven mindset, are an inseparable pair when considering life's accomplishments. I know that in my life, as a salesperson, some of the most important meetings in my business career I had in the mind, before I actually went to the meeting itself. I visualized what the other person would say about my products, I thought about the setting itself, and even anticipated some of the negative reactions that could result from the presentation I was about to give.

Have you ever thought about a really important person that you felt, if you could only meet them, your life would change forever? I want you to formulate at least three people in your mind who could do this for you – change your life, just from meeting them.

It could be a leader in your industry. It could be a leading coach or author - but no matter who it is, I want you to give thought to what would be said if you met these people. Think about the conditions that would need to occur in order for this meeting to take place.

Understand this, your desire and your ability to manifest this thought into reality in your mind, can be instrumental in accomplishing this goal. The most successful men that I have had the privilege of knowing, have all had this in common. Every single one is credited with bringing information into the world, from those who are ahead of them, and were doing it better than they are themselves.

Solomon was noted in the Bible as one of the wisest and richest men who had ever lived. He said repeatedly, that there was never anything new under the sun. What he meant was that all life is a duplication - in some form or fashion, of some event that has already occurred.

The Analogy of The Burning Ships

Nothing is new, but this does not mean there is no room for improvement. The point is, if someone is very far ahead of you in the conquest that you desire, they are often willing to share advice and concepts with you. You might even say that it is vital to the evolution of all things.

What your heart, body and mind desires is attainable, when you sit upon the shoulders of giants. Huge leaps are gained by meeting with people who have been successful in the areas you are looking to excel in. Many times in life, our desires are often sabotaged by leaving too many lifeboats available.

A warrior was once going to attack a great city. His boats were small, and the supplies were not plentiful. He knew he did not have enough men to execute a successful attack. When he and his men had finished unloading the boats, he gazed at the great walls surrounding the city. After a few moments, the warrior turned back and set all of the boats on fire. He knew in the path ahead, eliminating his means for failure was the only way he'd succeed.

Be sure that there are no outlets in your life that are quenching your desire. By nature, we as people are pleasure seekers, but pleasure in itself is not a great motivator - and can be a huge enemy of desire.

We all like good things, but when it comes to desire, and your motives for accomplishing greatness - pleasures alone must be cut away. If we are to have the desire we need to make greatness come to pass in our lives, there must be no complacency, no instant gratification, and no lifeboats we can escape on.

There is a statement that always resonates with me – 'starvation is motivation' and if I might add to that, 'save pleasure for victory.' When pleasure comes before victory, be very careful that you are not quenching your desire, and holding yourself back from the greatest victories that you can know in your life.

To define desire accurately, it is important to know that wishing, on its own, will not bring success. *Desiring* a specific level of success, means invoking a state of mind that borders on obsessive - with planning, specific goals and backing these goals with vicious persistence, which in no way recognizes failure. This will always bring you success. But first, you need to learn how to channel desire.

Finding Vision in Desire

Ancient wisdom says that a goal that doesn't have an effect on you, will not have an affect! You need to learn to channel desire in a positive way. If what you define as your goal doesn't inspire desire, make the goal closer to home. If you decide that your goal is going to be to sell 10 widgets - and this goal does nothing for you, change it.

These 10 widgets may get you 3 weeks of family vacation in the Caribbean (after charitable giving, savings, and life's demands of course) - and a trip to the Caribbean may mean time with the family, a special memory, and an awesome time of relaxation. If this really puts your 'coal in the engine' get this goal in front of you, and let no negative thought stop you from achieving it.

If you want that trip bad enough, do you know what you will do to get it? Anything! A goal that has the power to inspire life in you, is one of the most powerful chemical reactions that God has given us. Take the widget salesman for example. Let's say he changed his goal from the 10 widgets that his conscious mind tells him he wants, to a Caribbean trip - something that his whole being can buy into. Here is where the power starts.

The Widget Salesman puts a picture of the Caribbean, a powerful view of that beautiful powdery beach, with the crystal clear water, on the back of a small business card, and on the other side of that card, the words *"I can do all things through Christ who strengthens me"*.

I have several successful friends who do this, people who have made hundreds of thousands of dollars, and some millionaires, and I have seen phrases used such as "Every day I play like a Champion", or "Ask and it shall be given, seek and ye shall find, knock, and the door shall be opened unto you".

Visual affirmations do amazing things for a set goal. When you can see the end result, the reward of that hard work – it drives you on. Suddenly, you're not just selling 10 widgets anymore. You're on a mission to spend well deserved time with your family, to get that relaxation that you so desperately need. Uniting desires with your goals, means visualizing the impact of your actions. This reconstructs the bridge between desire and reality.

Feet From The Gold

Success starts within the mind. Your mindset is an incredibly powerful tool, that many people will never learn to harness in their lifetimes. When you have truly implanted an idea in your mind, it puts everything into motion. The most significant or insignificant, the great or the small, the harmful or the healthy, it all begins in the mind.

So many people confuse or miss opportunity when it knocks, and this is because it usually comes on the heels of a disappointment or setback! This is why it is so important to nurture a focused mind. The theory that one door closes and another opens, is true. The trick is not to sit down against the closed door in a heap, continuously refusing to check out the new door that's casting light at your feet.

One of the most defining features of a person that lacks success, is that they don't bounce back after a setback or negative event. In, *Think and Grow Rich*, Napoleon Hill gives us an incredible analogy to enhance this point.

A man caught 'gold fever' during the days of the gold rush out west, and decided to go claim his fortune in gold. He staked a claim and got to work, tirelessly digging day after day, with his fortune cemented in his mind. After many weeks of relentless digging with his shovel and pick, he struck gold. The only problem was, he had no machinery to bring it to the surface.

He returned home, and spoke to his relatives about getting the money together to buy the machinery. It was collected, and the machinery was shipped to his mine. They loaded a car with ore, and it was sent to the smelter.

The man believed he had found one of the richest mines in Colorado! A couple more cars and his debts would be paid, then he'd be rich.

He continued to drill, until suddenly the vein of gold vanished. No matter how hard he tried, he could not find it again. So, they cut their losses and sold the machinery to a junk man for a few hundred bucks. But this junk man was smart – very smart. Instead of selling the equipment, he hired an engineer to do some calculations in the mine. Based on fault lines that the miner didn't take into account, the engineer advised that the vein was merely three feet from where they were digging. And there it was.

The junk man pulled up millions from that mine, and all because he sought expert counsel before deciding to sell the machinery. The relative of the miner, a Mr. R.U. Darby, spent years paying back the money that his miner uncle had borrowed for the machinery. Long after that, Mr. Darby discovered that desire can be transmuted into gold. He learned from quitting when he was three feet from gold that it's never okay to quit, and as a result became a millionaire life insurance salesman.

Most people quit before success can strike. Not quitting, separates highly successful people from everyone else. Before the most climactic successes can be achieved, it is highly likely that a devastating setback, or a series of crises will befall you, and it's imperative that you push through them.

There are hundreds of accounts of successful men and women, whose greatest achievements were found just on the other side of an epic defeat. Fight on! Use setbacks, but never dwell on them. The successful achievements that we have enjoyed, only come to us as a result of the learning experiences gained from setbacks and defeats. Just look at R.U. Darby. He learned from his first experience in the gold mining business, and carried this lesson throughout his life.

As a result, he was an incredible success as an insurance salesman – never allowing his clients to say no when he offered them life coverage. By stopping three feet from the gold the first time, Darby learned that success is only attained through the combination of desire and stickability. Failure, he learned, is a trickster with a keen sense of irony and cunning. *Never quit.*

Perseverance and Lateral Thinking

Understand this in advance and be sure you are a student of the trials of life, in that you have done what you can to maneuver them successfully, should you engage them again. As long as I can remember, I was always told that hard work pays off. One thing that my parents never taught me, is that riches begin with a state of mind. I have met people who were some of the hardest working people that you will ever see, that always scraped by in life.

It's a shame that we all know many people in this position. I believe that we are either heavily 'success conscious' or we are 'failure conscious,' and some to the extreme. Whether we acknowledge it or not, or whether we have realized it in the past - our mind is constantly working with or against us – affecting our hard work, bringing us things that we want, and things that we don't want.

Often, our upbringing has a huge impact on stalling the improvement of our mindset. Our brain has taught us that we can expect a life of fear and anguish, misery, limitation and a life built from struggle. I believe you are made by a divine Creator to be whoever you want to be. But you must engage the battle of the mind, and combine it with hard work to achieve the success that you desire.

People that have had the most success in life, often have the disposition of a small child. I think of amazing people like Henry Ford, who one day, decided on a piece of paper - that he felt the engine should have an eight-cylinder engine block. Up until this point, Henry Ford's life had never been about a V8 motor. He simply went to the staff at Ford and demanded that this engine be created.

His workers and engineers looked at him and said, "Henry, you are absolutely crazy for even thinking that this is possible." But, Mr. Ford unflinchingly replied that he would have it anyway. As months and weeks dragged on, Henry unabashedly would come in and ask his men for updates. Many times these updates were met by confusion, when the men did not have a solution for creating Ford's engine.

But, you know what - Henry Ford did get his V8 engine. Sheer determination is the difference between a step, and a mile. The accomplishment that you desire however, must be gained in the mind first, to take its physical form within your life. That is success. That is victory. One of my favorite quotes from the mind of Napoleon Hill says, "*Whatever the mind of man can conceive and believe, it can achieve.*"

One of the greatest handicaps a person will ever experience, is how to apply dominating thoughts that align with their purpose.

Your thoughts must become magnetized, and every dominating motivation produced by the mind - should give birth to the success that you desire. No matter what it is, an accomplishment, eradication of an addiction, a specific monetary goal, or any given success in the areas of our lives.

Before you can accumulate anything, you must absolutely magnetize your mind with intense desire for this 'thing' in order for it to happen. Today is the day that you see yourself thriving in this area of your life. You may look at yourself in the mirror and see someone who is rather plain, but if you desire it – you can attain the rewards of kings. They will materialize in your life, and there is nothing in the physical realm that can stand in the way. Desire is the fuel that keeps your dreams alive.

Risks, Setbacks and Focus

What a world we live in today. It is amazing how many people, throughout various walks of life, have entered the ranks of billionaire. Have you ever thought of yourself as potentially becoming a billionaire? The wealthiest men that the world has ever been blessed to know, have unequivocally understood how to utilize the mind in the singular pursuit of success.

As far back as the Biblical times, desire, planning and focus have manifested critical aspects of success. *"For I know the plans I have for you, plans to prosper you, plans to give you hope and a future." – Jeremiah 29.11*

Men like Andrew Carnegie started out as just a standard laborer, and grew a fortune of hundreds of millions of dollars. Nearly everyone in the 20th century knew these truths and held to them.

Do you want to see an amazing turnaround in your family, or in a specific area of your life? Ask yourself how you can fan the flames of desire, for whatever it is that you want to achieve within your mind. Simply put, how big will you dare to dream? Imagine for a moment a young Thomas Edison, who lives in a world lit by flame and a lamp, and his pursuit to try to generate light with electricity.

Can you imagine the desire within a person who could fail 10,000 times, and still have the burning desire to manifest this idea into physical reality? It is easy to let negativity creep in. To accept your current circumstances. How big will you dare to dream? Surely, in your world, there are opportunities all around you. Areas waiting to be improved by a big thinker.

I am living proof of this. I grew up in a place of very limited means. But my parents encouraged me to dream big. That was the big difference for me, and it changed my life. I believed anything was possible if you wanted it badly enough. It turns out – the theory works!

Extreme Time Management

"No matter what you've done for yourself or for humanity,
if you can't look back on having given love and attention
to your own family, what have you really accomplished?"
- Lee Iacocca, Businessman and designer of the Ford Mustang

Success should not ruin our relationships. Be careful that you do not ruin your life in pursuit of noble causes. One can approach life with a singular purpose, and pay the ultimate price. Success is not measured in riches or fame, be wary or you might find yourself alone.

We often trade important people, for things that really don't mean a great deal at life's end. You might have a great car, but your spouse feels neglected and ignored. You might have an amazing career, but your friends and children don't know who you really are. It does not have to be this way. Victory and success are what we were designed for, but that does not and should not compromise the success we strive for in our personal relationships.

There are immutable laws that cannot be avoided in all areas of life. The weekend for example, comes directly from the Bible. The Hebrew's still adhere to this time. Traditionally the weekend is set aside for rest and worship, and begins from sunset on Friday, only ending on the full darkness of a Saturday night. It's known as Shabbat, and ensures that all of the Hebrew faith has time for recuperation. The word itself even means 'ceasing work.'

Giving 5, Taking 2

I am a driven Type A, dominating Alpha male who wants to win every day and work every day. I am the type of business person that like many of you, even when I am not working, my mind doesn't stop devising plans of what I will work on, when I am working again. If I am not near a computer, I will type notes on my phone, and if I am not near my phone, I will write a 'list' on anything I can find!

If left unfettered, I would never ever stop, and that just isn't fair to those that I care about, and those that care about me. What keeps my marriage strong, and adds to that ever-elusive balance, is that I give 5 and take 2. The concept is this: for 5 days of every week, I give my all to my businesses.

I mean this in the highest extreme. When I am going, I get up super early and I work super late. My workweek is a blur for 5 days, and my family and friends all know that this is the way it is. They also know that on the weekends, I will take 2 days off and give back to them.

I'm very serious about giving the 5 days your all. This is important – go all out. If you are employed, you absolutely crush it for 40 hours a week, and you don't stop there. If you want to be wealthy, 40 hours is just the start, and time that you invest to manage your basic needs. It's the time AFTER your 40 hours, where you really build your 'future.'

How much time after the 8-hour 'career' day do you work on your 'future' life? I would say at least 3 hours and 15 minutes. Additionally you should always get 45 minutes of physical exercise during all of this, and ideally, before the start of your 8 hour day. Then the additional future building period. That all stacks up to around 12 hours. Any more items added to this schedule will tend to give diminished returns, where the more you throw on, will not likely merit a relative payback.

If anything is shifted here, I recommend that as you are successful in your 'career' activities, you shorten your 'wage earning work day' down to 4 to 6 hours, and then give more time to the business you are creating. Wages provide a living, and profits provide for your dreams. There is a difference between wages and profits. The more profits you see from your 'future' or business related activities, the less wages or employee type activities you need to be involved in.

Planning Work and Play

As an employee, give 5 days a week to your boss, and to your future success, and take the last 2 and give them to your family. After a crazy workweek, it is imperative that you do this correctly, or you will still miss the mark in nurturing those that are close to you. Those of you who have successfully fired your boss already, are in business for yourselves. I have half of the earlier discussion covered. For you, the giving 5 is a common event.

No one has to tell you anything about 'showing up' and going hard until well after the sun has set. You may have some newfound freedom that your own business affords, but you know, that you never really 'unplug.' That is perfectly acceptable, and for seven days of every week, for now. You need to change your game plan, and do it now, before those that are close to you check out. Be careful. It may already be taking place.

Give your clients, your team, and your customers your very best self, for 5 days of every week and check out for 2 days. This means that the next time you hit the doors of your business, if you haven't done so, you analyze each day and you look at what it's like being your client or customer. Write out a set of Transaction Commandments. This is a set concept of what doing business with you is like. It means if being the very best is, a 3 hour turnaround, you do the thing in 2 hours.

If your business answers calls, and you know many are missed, you address the shortfalls in your team now. You look at your business through the lens of your customer, and you address the cracks from top to bottom.

After you have decided what the absolute highest standard looks like, you take 2 of the most practical days that can be had off, and do whatever you must to make sure that the business runs without your aid, for those 2 days. You also make sure that the Transaction Commandments are met as well as when you are actually on deck running your business.

Be smart about it – I have a good friend that is a Senior Pastor of a large church in Las Vegas. His time off, as you can guess, is not Sunday or Wednesday. Give the days you must and pick the 2 best options - and YES it's TWO, and you are going to take them. Believe it or not, the world will not slide off of its axis if you take 2 days off. It really won't!

Get rid of the excuses. There is no argument for trading away something that has everlasting value, for things that are temporal and at your graveside, meaningless. Think of life in the most appropriate sense – Sam Walton, the founder of Wal-Mart was a successful businessman, a billionaire when billionaires were unheard of.

Sam's family, are also billionaires as a result of Sam's dedication to so many. Funny thing though, when I pass away, in the afterlife, my personal self-worth here on earth is EXACTLY the same as Sam's! It's true no matter who you are! Warren Buffet, the Investment wizard of Omaha, has been one of the world's wealthiest investors – when he dies, we will share the same net worth on the day we both pass on.

What does go on, is far more valuable. Our name and legacy passed on through the love shared in our children. A lifelong pursuit to give our intellect and wisdom to the world, while being supremely noble, is no excuse to trade away the people in our life who are so special. Do not buy into the lie that you can't have a successful family, business, and wealth. Don't buy into the lie that you shouldn't have wealth as you have given something up to have it. This is not true. The Bible says, "The Love of" wealth is a "Root" cause of negative issues (paraphrase).

Wealth is evil WHEN YOU give away that which is special to pursue the wealth: Family, your good name, and your morals. The Bible describes many men who were extremely wealthy and yet special to God. The Bible's description of these men showed that they had wide success in life because of balance and their protection of what was important.

If you aren't having success, then you aren't taking 2 the way you should! I sit down with other business owners and managers, and as we round out a meeting, it is often an ideal time to exchange some personal thoughts. There are times, when a conversation will come up about the struggle with balance, and how they are not getting along with their spouses. In successful people, the root cause of this, is generally, that the person isn't really taking 2 days and giving it back!

Unplug Electronically

This is key! We often sit in front of a computer all day, and then get home and if we don't have a laptop out, will be on our cell phones trolling social networking sites like Twitter or Facebook! If tension is still high in your family, try an 'electronic fast!' Put it all down for 2 days and listen to your family! You will be amazed at what can happen and the response you will get.

Fact – 77% of the American population use the internet. Of this amount, 30% are between the ages of 18 and 32, 23% between 33 and 44, and 22% belongs to the 45-54 age demographic. Time spent on a PC is significantly higher, though the internet is the main reason for people to use a PC these days. Add this to the average TV watching stat of 4 hours per day, and the average time spent on cell phones, another 4 hours per day – and when does family time happen?

Ask Them

Find out what your wife, kids, or friends want to do! This is a great way to check in, so that they start thinking, "he or she's really back!" This may seem obvious, but we are successful people here! We have a plan for our days off, just as we do on the 5 days we use as a professional.

We can be so cheesy about our time off too. You say, "I am going to watch a movie with my kids," but you picked it out, and it's really something that they don't want to see. They are only sitting there because they love you and want to connect with you on some level for a change.

Dad and Mom, play the video game your kid wants to play, even though it will take you 3 weekends just to master the basic moves.

Guys, take your wife or friend out to the restaurant that they want to go to, without calling all of the shots. Go window-shopping after that, as painful as we know it will be.

Ladies, go out and attempt to manage even 9 holes of golf, or a tennis match with your husband. It will completely blow his mind, and I think it will be more fun than you can imagine.

Offload The Chores

Those of you that are ultra successful and those of you that have tasted a great deal of success, get rid of your to-do list by outsourcing it to a handyman, housekeeper, or lawn guy. You will find that your last week's dollar per hour, will double, triple, quadruple and go beyond what it would cost a skilled tradesperson, to manage your list. If you see yourself in this position pay wise, then it makes economic sense to pay someone else.

Why take a pay cut and an investment of time to work around the home, when someone else can do it. Time is the most important asset you have, it is precious and it is not something you can produce – you can only care for it, sculpt it, and manage it. The short explanation on how to manage time is "Do ONLY what you must do" and get rid of the rest!

I am teaching you to compress time, and push your earning potential to the max. You have to entrust people to do what they do best and focus on enjoying your family for two solid days.

By the way, letting your chores down, will hurt you at home. If you have roommates or family, having the care of your home slip will add a negative impact on you personally, and will harm your relationships. The mission of this book is to make developing people, success literate, and those that have a measure of success, develop an Extreme Mastery of Life.

Back To Desire

There is a transfer of mindset between setting a goal, dreaming something really big in the mind, and being ready in the physical world to turn that dream into reality. To be prepared to 'receive' in a physical sense, there is a switch away from a hope or magical dream, to a hard lined belief. This is the fire in one's self that comes from meditation, and constant affirmation. They help to transfer these thoughts into reality.

This too takes work. It doesn't take a LOT more work to create an ingrained belief, than it does to "HOLD ONTO" a poverty mindset, that dwells in a world of scarcity. Feeding this mindset is key. Our divine Creator has given us an amazing super computer that is installed above our shoulders, we use it very infrequently and to a very LOW degree, and to that end, we do ourselves a disservice in what we achieve as people.

We take care of cars, and boats, and worthless things that we 'acquire' but the things that we were 'born with,' are used and not cared for nearly as well! It's really crazy. How do we use our minds to create a powerful belief and culture burning desire? Think of it this way: The story you tell yourself creates a picture in your mind. The mind then goes to work at physically creating and manifesting the picture that YOU fed it!

If you tell your kids, they can win the spelling bee, then don't be surprised if they manifest that story! If you tell yourself, everything I eat turns to fat, (so I might as well have the pizza) - then you are destined to struggle with weight. This is a huge problem with business people. In the 1990s and first decade in 2000s, we have seen a historical range of economic swings.

Times are great, then times are horrible. This has an incredible impact on everyone from top to bottom. We exist in a negative society, and as a result, when the changes go badly, people get very depressed. Our lives, business, and jobs, are either good or bad, based on the movie that we have playing between our ears. It's true! I know immensely successful business owners, whose industry completely disappeared in this time.

The ones who had superior control over the mind, got through it by being in total control of their mind set. What did they do? They focused immensely on what it was that they wanted, and avoided thinking that did not support their ultimate goals. When times would get really tough, these men and woman would start their day or end their day, with a mental 'yoga session' to make sure they didn't relapse to the negative thought patterns.

Mental Yoga

There is a point in each day, where there was a focused effort of at least 10 minutes of time, where the mind was completely emptied of all thoughts, all concerns, and all negativity. Additionally, these successes managed an additional 10 to 20 minutes of prayer and meditation.

Ideally, this is done in the morning, alone, before anyone in the house is up. Or is done at night by walking alone. This is extremely powerful especially in challenging times, because distractions have a weird way of taking up much more 'space' in your mind.

When you get quiet in meditation, you allow those 'spaces' to clear, so that the positive, innovative dreams can again consume our minds and bring into focus the things which should occupy space within us. Additionally, through prayer and meditation, you speak your issues out. You ask for support for those particular issues and you come away with a sense that you have a powerful ally on your side - God.

This brings a new dynamic to failure. Edison was said to have failed 10,000 times before the light bulb was created. When he was on the 9,990th failure, do you think he knew that he was 10 failures away from success? No. He didn't know if he was 9,990 failures STILL away from his dream! He could only see that one failure, but God sees where we are in life, whether we are only a few failures away from our dream, or whether we are 1,000 failures from it.

Understand, that when a door closes, another door opens. This is a cheesy old analogy, but it does indicate that we have to keep at it. When a new chapter of life begins, or the proverbial 'other door opens,' there is a new fire in us, a burning desire that is rekindled. Instead of sulking, you have to be vigilant about pulling every ounce of energy you have, kicking yourself in the butt, and as tenaciously as if we were operating on the last day of our life, to find that open door! That is the goal. During this period of time, it's hugely important that you focus all of your energy to restore that mental picture. The one that tells the story of the victory that you will be achieving, as you approach that open door. Once again, this is done through the daily 'Yoga Session' of the mind! Both success and failure are the offspring of thought! Mastery of your own mind is going to change your life. Believe it.

The Amplification of Desire

Now, you need to learn to amplify your desire. Here's how.

1. Define your goal – use specifics. If you have a business and a specific revenue goal, set that goal in an ideal figure (example

1 million in sales). This is incredibly important for your mind to adopt and put into play the success that you desire.

2. Define the services that you will render to bring about the goal that you have set!

3. Define a specific date for the goal that you are working towards.

4. Develop a written plan that will define exactly how you will bring about the success that you will achieve. It's highly important that you begin this particular point, even if you have every detail of that plan worked out at the moment you sit down to write. This very act of initiating a written plan immediately starts to bring about the steps, which must mentally take place to bring about the physical aspects that you desire.

5. Write out a more elaborate, clearly detailed plan on the services that you will render - the steps that you must take, and the personal developments and habits that must be acquired, to fully carry out and achieve the goals you've set yourself.

6. If you pray or meditate, take your plan and pray over not only written goals, but your plan to achieve those goals. Ideally do this three times a day - but a minimum of twice today, to see your goals taking place with clarity in your mind.

The six steps are equally important. Those with ambition are trained to write a defined set of goals. We are taught that we are to write the goal out, and set aside the details of that goal. Sadly, we're never taught how to fully bring to ourselves the aid of our minds, in pursuit of accomplishing this goal. Ancient wisdom says, master the power of desire, and you shall have it all.

CHAPTER THREE

THE WISDOM OF FAITH

What lies behind us and what lies before us are tiny matters compared to what lies within us

– Ralph Waldo Emerson

The Fuel That Sets Your Life Aflame

Ancient wisdom reminds us to develop the infinitely powerful beliefs that can allow us to be better people, lovers, businessmen, leaders, or countrymen. Faith is the basis of all focus, passion and desire.

What's the point of wanting something, when you don't believe you can make it happen? In this context, faith is the fuel that will set your life aflame. It gives you the strength to persevere, through any adversity. It's the hero mindset, the rocket fuel that drives action.

Many psychologists claim that love, sex (appeal), and faith are the most powerful of the positive emotions that one experiences. These three emotions can collectively tap subconscious thoughts in a very powerful way - so much so, that when applied to a thought impulse, they can drive it to greater action than any of these emotions can do singly.

Much like we discussed in the Ancient Wisdom of Desire, thoughts that are turned over to emotion, or have feeling added by faith, begin to immediately transform themselves into the physical equivalent.

You build a picture in your mind through self-affirmations or 'stories.' When desire is applied, your mind creates the picture, and through faith, these mere thoughts start to root and develop in your life. You could say that faith is the battery that charges desire, and desire the mechanism for positive visual goals.

Education and Success

Mastering this alone will create amazing success in your life. Some people have mastered it, but only have 'faith' in a life of inadequacy, scarcity, and poverty. How many times have you heard absolute beliefs slip from your mouth? "There is not enough money!", "I'm not qualified enough to be successful," "I'm too fat to look good," or "I can't risk losing that money."

I personally know many successful people, who had no ivy league education (no college at all for that matter), BUT they knew about Ancient Wisdom, Universal Laws, and specifically, how to master the mind to channel this amazing super computer to drive the physical manifestations into their life, in incomprehensible amounts.

Achievement begins in our minds. It's simply not about what we have access to, or what we have accomplished to date. Consider this again, that *any* thought or goal that has been emotionalized through desire, or realism, when faith is added, will start to manifest and come to pass in the physical sense.

This is powerful because it leads to negative or positive occurrences in our lives. Later on, we will discuss the mind and its role in guiding us, either to things we want, or to things that we don't want. Most people end up struggling for a lifetime, with emotions and realities that they don't want - because they have no clear idea on how to manipulate thoughts, emotions, and faith to bring about amazing events and a life ful of success.

Ancient Wisdom must be utilized for all of these things to be achieved. Desire, as was discussed earlier, heavily influences our conscious mind on a daily basis. On a small scale, we're great at feeding this desire. You want an ice cream, so you go out and get one. This is possible without faith. On a larger scale, however, it's just not possible. That's where we fall short.

Our conscious mind is the 'operator' aspect of our mind. Faith, however is the deeply ingrained belief system in ourselves that powers our subconscious. There is a lot more information in society available, on how to manage the conscious 'operator' portion of our brains, but it's the 'subconscious' or the 'secret agent' portion of our minds, that really produces life changing and amazing results.

Our 'inner dialogue' shapes our faith and our beliefs. It's just as easy to derail a negative self-dialogue, by speaking positively on the outside. The theory is commonly called autosuggestion and is similar to hypnosis. You must 'suggest' good things to yourself, to replace your negative belief system.

If you feel that you can't overcome your current surroundings to be successful – you would say, *"I am a success. I am a champion, and every day, I will play life, like a champion."* If you feel like there isn't enough in your life, or that prosperity is limited for you, you would say, *"There is money everywhere in the world, lots of it. I am going to be my best self, and serve others at a high level, so that I will receive at very high levels."*

If you feel like your current world is waning, that your job is diminishing or your business is failing, say *"My Creator takes care of all of my needs. When one door closes, another one opens, and a great opportunity is around the corner. I will be positive and ready for the next amazing turn that life has for me today".*

Faith And Goal Achievement

Our faith is key. In fact, our Creator knew that faith was important, and He established promises that we could trust in, to make sure that we applied Faith in all things.

> *I tell you the truth, if you have faith as small as a mustard seed, you can say to this mountain, 'Move from here to there' and it will move.*
> Matthew 17:20

The basis for our faith is key, because of the ancient laws of attraction. If we are looking for positive things, our life will be positive. Opportunities will abound, and we will be in the appropriate mindset to receive them. We have a sense when we are positive, that our network of human support is with us on our endeavor, and helps us to meet our goals. Just the opposite is true with negative people. If you are negative, then you will attract negativity. Opportunities will close to you, people in your network will shun and run from you, and doors will close.

It doesn't matter what happens in life, if you are breathing air, then you have a world of opportunities.

Steve Jobs was born as an adoptee, dropped out of college, was fired from his own company, later rehired, and died an admired leader, visionary and innovator. He also changed the world with new technology, namely the iPhone, iPad and iPod. But most of all, he gave us the graphical interface computer – the very foundation of all online interaction today.

Abraham Lincoln had limited schooling, put himself through law school, experienced close family deaths, and bankruptcy - which back in those times, was very stigmatized, and became President. He went on to become a significant influence in the world, when he abolished slavery in America, freeing millions of people.

Richard Branson, born to a middle class family in London, suffered from dyslexia and dropped out of high school, started his own business at the age of 16, grew it into a massive corporation, and became the 254th richest person in the world. He is most noted for his humanitarian efforts, and has supported dozens of worthy causes in his lifetime.

Mark Zuckerberg, born to a middle class family, has red-green colorblindness, excelled in school, dropped out of Harvard on the invention of Facebook, is now personally worth over 17 billion dollars, though still struggles with lawsuits and the media. He has given millions to education foundations and has pledged to give half of his wealth to charity.

Walt Disney, born into a working class family, was fired from his first newspaper job for not having enough 'imagination,' started several businesses that went bankrupt and failed, then founded Walt Disney Productions and enjoyed enormous success, wealth and influence. During his lifetime, he gave selflessly to many philanthropic causes.

Poverty is Not an Excuse

There are countless more examples of this, so the argument can't be broken! There is no reason why EVERY opportunity that can be had, shouldn't be had by you. The ONLY difference is this: The world is open or closed to you based on your view of it in your mind. There is enough money, for you and your business, available, and enough for a bountiful estate for your kids, their kids, and their kids too, if you believe the right things.

All of life's problems are either opportunities or issues, and it all starts in the 4 inches between your ears. Waking up happy every day is a choice, and it really is as simple as that. It's right there, in front of us - and is no more complex than that. The reality is that we live in a negative world!

We have to actively feed our belief system every single day with positive feedback. We have to reinforce our dreams as actively as we pursue good food! You should discourage negative thoughts, with just the same vigor.

People actually seem to prefer being grouchy and negative. Don't you sometimes feel that way? Reality is hard. But you create your own reality, you really do.

In a competitive world, negativity is a horrible approach. Those with a sound control over their beliefs, and are producing action from a positive placement through faith, will not have a very large challenge in moving ahead in any given field.

Advice and Opportunity

Have Faith in what you can do, and have Faith in a Creator that has supplied you with all of the tools you need to succeed. Faith, once again, is the 'magic fuel' that gives life, power, and action to our thoughts. This sentence needs to be repeated!

Faith is the starting point of material success, and wealth as well. It's the beginning point of all 'miracles' and mysteries that science itself has no answers for!

Faith is the only known remedy for failure. Faith is the product, the system which, when mixed with prayer, gives one direct communication to a Divine Intelligence.

How do you harness positive thought? How do you have faith that compels your actions in appealing ways, over negative ones? Start with overriding your current self-dialogue, with a new, more positive language.

Did you know that if you repeat a lie over and over to yourself, you will literally start to buy into the lie as a truth? Politicians use this one all the time. They campaign for votes based on chatter, talk and blatant lies. Yet, ask any politician, and they will tell you that they believe their campaign promises, even years after they have not materialized. Eventually, a lie repeated that often, solidifies as truth in their minds.

Thoughts that have emotion behind them become magnetized, transform into an overriding power in the body, and are able to attract additional similar thoughts as well. Basically put, once you put the right rocket fuel in, a chain reaction begins. This doesn't seem all too easy upfront, but as with anything, the effort will pay off.

Start with strict focus, and imagine that your life is a house. If you were building your mind and your beliefs, what would this building look like? Throw off all of the distractions of your current reality. What beliefs are currently shackling you? Do you struggle with timidity or self-confidence?

Are you barred by vicious anxiety or poor self-esteem? These can be powerfully overturned by the simple act of daily suggestion, a new 'truth' introduced, and a new faith driving the powerful subconscious mind to work for you, and not against you.

Here is a sample suggestion for inspiring self-confidence from faith.

1. I believe I have the ability to obtain any goal or any obstacle. I have the willpower to achieve, and will persist to completion, with all of my heart.

2. I know that my beliefs are the driving forces for the actions that I desire, and that every day for 30 minutes, I will focus intently and quietly on the beliefs that will be required, to produce the person that I want to become.

3. I know that through constant suggestion, that whatever I hold within my mind, will manifest itself in my life in the physical sense, and I will spend 15 minutes a day demanding and devoting myself mentally to make myself self-confident.

4. I am clear on who I am and where I want to end up. I have properly defined my best self, and I will not stop developing 'self confidence' until I have attained this goal.

5. No manner of wealth or success can be gained without a mutual win, or success of the person that I am exchanging goods with. I will not engage in any transaction where both parties can't come away a success, or where one party will come away harmed. I will eliminate negative thinking. I will not focus on anything other than what will serve my best self. I will repel anger, negativity, jealousy, and moral degradation from my thinking and from my network of support. I am committed to reviewing this statement every day, will commit this to memory, and will sign my name to it. I know that my belief patterns are already changing and that faith is already guiding me to

develop self-confidence, and all traits needed to be an independent successful person.

Faith In a Higher Power

At face value, you might not see a process like this, as worthy of your time. Imagine that the seeds of your greatest success, and most creative imagination, are locked within you - waiting to be released and put to good use.

They are already there, but not likely aiding you – they're working against you. Your ability to be successful in using the powerful process of suggestion, will depend on your ability to focus on a given desire until the point that it becomes a burning obsession.

Being specific is another process that will help in bringing this process to life. As an example, if you desire a sum of money, state the amount and state the amount of time that you have to make this happen. Define in detail the services that you will provide, in order to achieve what it is you desire. In this instance, if you aren't clear on what the service is that you will render, do not force this aspect.

The subconscious will aid you in bringing to mind what this service should be, so that you can achieve all that you desire. This will generally come in a flash of inspiration, or a hunch.

Once you have established what the service will be, and the quantity of this service, you must start visualizing your process of rendering some. This is very important. Faith is ignited as this visual is drafted over and over in the mind, and is once again the chemical 'elixir.' You will need it to drive the thoughts and actions required to fulfill what you have asked of yourself.

The Mind Gym

I like to think of this as a mind gym. Just as a powerful swimmer must train for hours a day, or a runner must hit the track, we must spend time developing our state of mind.

You see, the subconscious mind, the 'secret agent,' is working within you, and it makes no distinction between a good story or a bad one. The subconscious is much like a heat-seeking missile - and it acts only in one process. It takes coordinates, and fires off actions - whether they're negative and destructive, or success driven.

The fact remains, that we are not trained to know how to modify the coordinates of this system. The programming that we are receiving on a daily basis, from the world around us, is VERY negative, and sabotages us often. The process of autosuggestion is the process of re-writing the coordinates that our mind is receiving, and restructuring our belief system to not work against us, but for us.

Faith has the powerful effect of persuasion as well, on others. Have you ever heard someone try to convince you to buy something, when you know that their process of encouraging you to buy into their product, didn't come from a place of faith in the product? Hundreds of millions have been earned when people buy in. Dreams come to reality when faith is behind what a person is selling.

Charles Schwab

Charles Schwab is a great example of this. At the tender age of 31, he was appointed president of Carnegie Steel Company. As a result, he helped sell Carnegie Steel to JP Morgan, a New York based financier, and became president of the new company – US Steel.

On December 12, 1900, Schwab met with JP Morgan and a host of other industrialists to discuss an idea that he had. They didn't know then that it would become the most significant meeting in American industrial history. Schwab gave a passionate speech that resonated with his audience. But more than that, it was well planned, fully executable; and a fantastic idea - unite small inefficient steel companies to create one large mega-company that runs on the same principles.

It was a risky business, and JP Morgan refused several other steel companies before him. But his passion and faith eventually won out. US Steel eventually, went on to become a giant corporation, worth 600 million dollars in the early 1900s. A combination of desire, faith and tenacity made it possible.

Riches themselves, success in any venue of life - begin in a single mode of thought.

This is an ideal time, to give some thought to the mind itself. First, there is conscious thought. This is where you knowingly operate from on a daily basis. If you decide to stop and get gas for your car, or determine that you are having a salad for lunch, you likely obtained this from conscious thought.

Then, there is subconscious thought, and this is the more mysterious and amazing area for the person who knows how to tap into it. Your subconscious mind will operate when you sleep, or operate involuntary mechanisms in the body, such as breathing. This amazing part of you works nonstop and when tapped, can be your onboard navigation, to take you to places you never thought possible. Have you ever had a hunch? Have you ever had a problem that you didn't have a logical answer for immediately - but then 2 days later, out of the blue, a solution popped into your mind?

The subconscious mind was not known as the 'marvelous' target seeking mechanism that it is today - until the 1950s. Oddly, at the same time, scientists were fascinated with the development of 'electronic, man-made brains' and through much of this revolution, brought about today's knowledge of how powerful our subconscious really is.

In the most basic sense, our 'goal striving' mechanism, the 'subconscious' is used to help us live. The real power is learning how make this super computer serve us, in accomplishing more than we could ever dream. Animals too have a 'goal striving' mechanism. For instance, a squirrel does not have to be raised and taught to find and consume nuts. A bird doesn't have to go to a trade school to learn nest building - but it can do it.

A bird does not have to grab a newspaper or catch the weather channel to divert course in order to avoid dangerously cold weather. In our attempt to make these explanations we generally mention 'instincts.' These instincts give the animal the guidance they need to successfully manage situations in the wild, in order to live. In short, the animal has a 'success striving' mechanism.

One thing that is often overlooked, is that man was also created with 'instincts' or 'success striving mechanisms', but our Creator in no way short changed us by comparison. Animals can't manipulate goals, where man can.

An animal has a 'preset' or 'preloaded' pattern of survival. Man on the other hand, has creative imagination. This makes man more than a creature, but a creator as well. With our imagination, we can formulate all sorts of goals and dreams. Using the power of the subconscious mind, faith, desire and focus – you can live every goal you ever set for yourself, to completion. You only need to learn to condition your mind to accept the positive, and reject negativity.

To embrace change and innovation, and to always be on the lookout for the next opportunity. Do this and you will condition your mind to become a success machine. Remember – faith is the fuel that drives desire!

The Amplification of Faith

- Faith is the belief in yourself, and the belief that God is watching over you, in everything you do.

- When you nurture self-confidence and divine faith, you are filled with courage, determination, perseverance and the inability to admit defeat.

- Faith adds emotion to your visions, giving you the power to achieve your desires and goals – as they manifest in reality.

- Faith is gained or lost according to your mindset. A negative mindset will discourage faith, while a positive one only makes it stronger.

- Change your negative mindset into a positive one. Change the way you speak to yourself, by adding positive affirmations to your internal dialogue. The only way to change your belief system, is to adapt how you talk to yourself.

- Faith is reliant on both the conscious and subconscious minds. Your conscious mind operates while you are awake, but your subconscious mind never stops working. Filter positive affirmations to your subconscious mind by training your conscious thoughts. Eventually your goals will be aligned, and every part of your amazing cognitive ability working towards a single purpose – your success.

- Put your faith in God, always. He will never give you more than you can handle. And it's often in these times of trial, tragedy or despair that real opportunities arise. When you live with faith, your mind will be programmed to spot them, and you'll see that second door open.

Continue to work on your attitude every day. I can't formulate a sentence powerful enough to reinforce this statement. It is vital that you learn to master your thoughts. If you do not, you will find success far more difficult to achieve.

CHAPTER FOUR

THE WISDOM OF THOUGHT

> *A pessimist sees the difficulty in every opportunity; an optimist sees the opportunity in every difficulty.*
> *– Winston Churchill*

Some of the greatest minds that ever contributed to the world discovered the importance of thought and perspective well before they became great. Many of them found that the way your mind works is directly related to the success that you achieve in life. I believe that your mind is where greatness begins.

Positive Thinking

If you are prone to thinking negatively about the world, about your life in particular, then you are limiting your potential. Limits are an interesting concept. Positive thinking teaches us that there are no limits, as long as your mind is focused and open and you are willing to push forward.

Yet, we are taught from a very young age that the world is limited, that there is only so much that we can do or achieve as people.

After all, "You're only human." These expressions and deep-seated beliefs are nothing more than a way to comfort yourself when you give up. When you learn to think positively about your actions – mistakes and successes – you're motivated to move forward. People who are able to overcome disappointment and negative limitations eventually do succeed. When something bad happens, they learn from it and make adjustments to their plans.

Society tells us success is virtually unachievable, especially when you come from poverty or bad circumstances. If this is true, why do so many of the world's most successful people come from humble beginnings? The only answer is that they understood the power of positive thinking. Sometimes this is an innate sense, ingrained in bright minds that are obsessed with a singular goal.

We call them geniuses, but really, they are just people who refused to admit failure. Michael Jordan, the world's most famous basketball player, was dropped from his high school basketball team. It was a setback yes, but the disappointment did not crush him. Many children would have found something else to do. Instead, Jordan kept playing and worked harder than anyone else to become a superb basketball player.

JK Rowling, the billionaire author of the famous Harry Potter books, was rejected by 12 mainstream publishing houses before Bloomsbury finally accepted her book for publication. If she had not pushed forward, the world would never have come to love Harry Potter as they did. It is still the fastest selling series ever published, with an estimated 500 million fans all over the globe.

In both Michael Jordan's and JK Rowling's case, positive thinking fueled their desire to be successful and to never give in to defeat. Life is like that –it will throw you curve balls and knock you down. What you choose to do after you have seen failure dictates your future.

All positive thinkers in the world ignore what society has taught them. These positive thinkers are relentless in their pursuit of success, and will not stop until they achieve success.

Ancient wisdom says that positive thinking is the path to true happiness in your life. This is because you are constantly anticipating the successful outcome of your actions. It frees you from limitations and opens your mind to new possibilities.

What's the Difference?

A negative mindset is ready to accept failure, anticipating it on the horizon. A man who has just gone bankrupt, after years of attempting to run a business, will usually give up and do something else. Bankruptcy is the failure notice. This man will accept that his attempts have failed, and that he was obviously not very good at it. If this man had a positive mindset, he would open another business.

Taking note of all the things that went wrong the first time, he would carefully ensure that they did not happen again. By applying the lessons he learned from his failed business, his chances of being successful the second time round are much greater. Society teaches us that failure is shameful, embarrassing and wrong. But it's not – it is educational, enriching and inspiring.

If Thomas Edison had not failed 1,000 times before creating the first working light bulb, he may not have felt the need to push as hard as he did for success. Positive thinking turns negative experiences into great lessons. When your mind is geared to be positive, it boosts your self-esteem and enhances your talents. It also has an uncanny way of affecting the people around you. When you are positive, it inspires others to be positive as well.

To a person with a positive mindset – failure does not exist. This is because failure in its purest definition is the end of something. If there is no end, there is no failure. Imagine living in a world where failure really isn't an option. It takes all the risk out of life. If you do not feel like you are going to fail, you will not stop until you succeed. This is the most direct path to success.

You need to change your attitude towards yourself and towards your life. There is no such thing as perfection – in fact, life is littered with speed bumps and different paths that try to pull you off course. The men and women who succeed are the ones who stay on their chosen paths, even though they have every reason to give up. Your positive mindset will change your life. The question is, how will it change your life.

Planting the Seeds of Success

Do your planning and prepare your fields before building your home. I like to say, "Cash is king and credit is crack!" We live in a society that says go out and get whatever you want, and have it now. We break down wealth into monthly payments! If we go and buy a TV, that TV isn't $550, its $26 a month.

We pay for everything on time, and we are slaves to our credit ratings. Credit is the crack of the 20th and 21st century. When we see financial damage to the economy, most folks lose their precious credit score and the national average for saving goes up, and people actually buy things with cash, rather than financing it for a lifetime payment.

Ancient wisdom says that you must build your fields first, and then lay the foundation.

This is amazing, and it's a law of divine intelligence passed down to us. We do not prepare our fields first before the luxuries of life; we do it backwards. America is broke because of it, and Americans do not get everything that they can get from life. It's really sad. Our culture teaches us to do it backwards. Instant gratification now - worry about the money later. Things for free!

Marketing can have a very negative influence on your ability to grow financially. The business of marketing itself is a very serious business at this point. The business of creating something seductive or provocative, as to cause collective consumer action is actually called 'viral' marketing. TV is literally built on interrupting your life. It's really nuts! I have sat through dissertations from the smartest marketers on the planet, and they actually use the word 'interrupt' when a commercial flashes on the screen and gets into your mind in the middle of your busy day.

Unfortunately, I have this phrase 'interruption' programmed into my mind about commercials themselves, and I can't think of anything more mind numbing than someone literally stopping my train of thought for three to five minutes to convince me to buy their product. As a result, I have TiVo or DVR, do not watch live TV and have not done so in several years. If my wife wants to turn on a show that is not recorded, we will get into a little argument or she will record it live and we will watch something else.

But the point is that advertisers are serious about getting your attention, and that attention isn't always positive - for good reason. Remember those little distractions that pull you off your destined path? Commercial breaks are one of them.

Designers of products and their marketing components realized that for you to be appropriately 'interrupted' or impregnated with a productive 'virus', they have to make the product have a very high sex appeal.

This starts with our kids! They watch thousands of breakfast cereal ads that make them think that they can run through walls, if they eat a particular brand. Or they see toy commercials that make them feel 'part of the group' if they buy a particular toy. Now, we have grown ups that grow up, and do what? Develop negative eating habits and choices, and buy toys that they cannot afford! Listen and write this down: If you choose to live like no one else, then you will live, be and have like no one else.

Worry about your fields first, and then build your house. Grasping this, will aid in your success like nothing else in the world will, and that is because it is law. The first step to positive thinking is to pull your mind out of this consumer rut. Being concerned for your fields first, means getting a pad built up of emergency funds. Once you have emergency funds, build savings. Build yourself a pad so that if you get into trouble, six months could go by and you could still support yourself.

As you go, build up to a year. You have prepared the field for crops at this point, but GET THIS - real crops do not come until you have planted seed, and the seed I am talking about is money. Money really is the seed of success. The problem with most Americans is that they do not plant the seed; they take it to the market and trade it for Big Macs and Chevy Trucks! What the wealthy know that you do not is that the seed returns fruit, and from the fruit you build the house. You do not trade hard work for cheeseburgers, new couches and wide screen televisions.

You do not buy what you cannot really afford.

The secret of the seed is this - when you put those dollars, those seeds into the ground, and you do it wisely, an amazing thing happens. You see, when one apple tree seed goes into the ground, you do not get one apple from the one seed, you get a LOT of apples. In addition, you get them year after year, as long as you look out for disease from the tree.

When one seed goes into the ground, you get fruit from that seed, again, and again, and again, forever. Even your kids can eat the apples and their kids too! When you exchange the seed for a Big Mac or a Chevy, the Big Mac is gone, and the truck will overheat and break down well before your kids are old enough to drive it.

It is a selfish thing to not plant seed. It is more selfless to put as much as you can in the ground, and it will not only serve those after you, but also be a safety net for you as long as you are alive.

The world is very distracting. It's not good business to tell you to 'hey, save your money' - build your crops and then enjoy the finer things in life. But that's the real pathway to long term success with money, and we don't get it.

All it takes is one seed. Once you have planted it, everything in your life will automatically become easier. Success will be in reach. Opportunities will arise. Tell yourself every day, *"I am disciplined; I can do it, and I am going to shrink my lifestyle and forgo all of the silly distractions to get to where I really want to be in life."* In the end, you will have something long term and something real.

Another ancient proverb says, *"Those who love pleasure will become poor; those who love wine and luxury will never be rich."*

Fads are fads – the people who carry a $400 handbag on TV to walk the red carpet did not even have to pay for it to carry it.

Yet, we have people who barely earn $400 a week, working 30 to 40 hrs of their life - to pay for that purse! There is a time for the finer things, but first plant the crops. If you have tied yourself down with debt, get free of it now. Do not put it off, join the fight. Cash is king – credit is crack. Time for rehab!

Staying Positive in a Negative World

Most of our negativity comes from the fact that we never have money. Getting rid of your debt can free you from this crushing mindset. Have you ever noticed that powerful need for a new item that drives you to buy it – even though you cannot afford it? Then, once you have it – it's suddenly not that interesting anymore, and the next item fills your thoughts. The act of buying on credit is a negative thing.

Think about the reasons you dash out to buy something new - to look nice, to have a bigger TV, because you feel like you deserve a new lounge suite. These are all ridiculous reasons. But that's the age we live in. Instead of needing things, we want them – and want always wins the race. That is why you would rather spend thousands on a new car than replace your broken dishwasher.

When you do not have money, you feel stuck, frustrated and isolated. Suddenly all of your money is going to payments, and you barely have any to live on. In the real world, buying more useless things LOWERS your standard of living. Before your new car, you could afford to eat out twice a week. Now, you can only go on the rare occasion. Do you see how destructive credit is? Negativity fuels negativity, and deprivation causes more buying.

The problem is that no matter how much you buy – it does not make you happy. You have done nothing real with your life, and achieved no real success. You have just been scraping by – existing instead of living. Buying is not fulfillment. True success and fulfillment comes when you can buy without debt, and not have to experience the stress of making your payments each month.

To stay positive in this negative world, it is imperative that you free yourself from debt. Too much debt will strangle your ideas and impose harsh limitations on any opportunities that come your way. This does not mean that you cannot succeed with debt – of course, you can. Henry Ford went bankrupt five times before he succeeded. But, if you want to make it easier to change from a negative to positive mindset, then money can't be a constant stress. Scale down, and to heck with what people might think! You will benefit more in the long run.

Your Perspective Is Your Life

Ancient wisdom says, *"Don't wear yourself out trying to get rich. In the blink of an eye, wealth disappears."*

Many people drive themselves into the ground, working tirelessly for money. But money is not everything - it should be treated as a means to an end, not the end itself.

Most of us want to be rich, and we try hard to get there. But being wealthy is not a goal in itself, and it certainly doesn't solve any problems in life. In fact, many wealthy people have said that life was happier when they were poor. It is wonderful to achieve wealth, but this should be a byproduct of your original goal.

It is downright dangerous to have nothing but wealth embedded in your mind. It often causes you to exclude the things that really matter – such as family and friends. You forget to be giving, to help others, and instead pursue the selfish goal of collecting more and more money. It is quite ridiculous actually.

Because so many people are in crippling debt, and never try to resolve that problem – more money just leads to more debt. When you get a raise, you go out and buy more stuff on credit.

This is not a good perspective to live with, especially when the things that truly matter are being sidelined. Always remember that a giving heart and time spent with the people in your life are more valuable than money.

Have you been working late? On weekends? Doing more than a single person is ever supposed to do? Then you've gone off the path. Not only are you working towards a monetary goal that will never happen because of your debt, you are letting life pass you by.

In the blink of an eye, wealth can disappear. What will your life be measured by then? These are the things you need to work on. To be a positive thinker, you need to have the correct perspective on your life. Money is not everything, and it does not bring you happiness. If you really think about the end results of having money – you will find that it's often to spend more time with your family, go on holiday or really experience life to the fullest.

But you can do that now! Working to be wealthy does not mean putting the rest of your life on hold. Life happens. So, to truly become a positive thinker, your wealth needs to grow with your relationships. There has to be a balance. Or at the end of the road, when you do make money – you'll be alone. No amount of money will be able to replace the people you have lost.

A positive perspective will cure you of all the negativity that has kept you from achieving your potential. It involves the acknowledgement of all the good things in your life and the decision to see opportunity – even if comes from a terrible defeat. When you practice maintaining a positive perspective, you will find your self-worth skyrockets. You will cope with things better, and the people around you will become a comfort, instead of a frustration.

The Five Myths That Determine Your Perspective

Have you ever wondered why we see things the way that we do? Why we believe in certain paths, and ignore others? Our perspectives are based on who we are, and what we have experienced in our lives. To change the way we think, from negative to positive, we must acknowledge that these foundational beliefs are false.

The first comes from society, as many beliefs do. We are expected to achieve, and anything less than total success is regarded as a failure. If we don't always prove to be the pillars of success that society demands, its leads to a negative mindset.

The joke of course, is that no one is perfect. You are bound to make hundreds of mistakes, in every aspect of your life. But great men are respected because of their positive traits, not because of their lack of faults.

The second is the belief that if something threatens you, or terrifies you; you must constantly worry about it. Worry and anxiety are the precursors of failure, as they force you to eventually shut down from exhaustion. There is no point worrying about an outcome, a person or an event. The key is to let things happen as they do, then deal with problems as they arise. To be consumed with fear is a large part of sustaining a negative mindset. Positive people are naturally fearless.

Third is the consistent need for approval from those around you. We are brought up to thrive on praise, and when we do not get it, there is an intense feeling that something's wrong. When you hinge your behavior on the opinions of others, it makes for an incredibly rocky ride.

People are naturally self-absorbed, and rejection is a part of life. To gain a positive mindset you must begin to trust yourself, and stop making bad decisions based on the opinions of others.

Fourth is the belief that your past dictates your future. While we have many experiences that have made us who we are, they can be changed. You do not have to be a slave to your past mistakes, and gaining a positive mindset will free you from this burden. Instead, live in the moment and plan for the future. It is always better to strive to be someone you admire in the future than to hang onto who you were in times past.

Finally, the belief that your emotions depend on outside circumstances, things such as money, where you work, live, even the car you drive. These external circumstances do not define you as a person, but they can make you feel inadequate. Cast away this belief, and adopt a positive mindset, and you will see that your emotional wellbeing does not depend on 'things' or 'people' but how you behave in your own life.

These five beliefs cripple people, and force them to adopt a permanently negative mindset that holds them back. You need to shake free of these beliefs and fill yourself with new hope on a daily basis.

All things are possible with a positive mindset and God's help. When the weight of the world is on your shoulders, you can always find strength and happiness knowing that He is on your side.

The Amplification of Positive Thought

"The positive thinker sees the invisible, feels the intangible and achieves the impossible."

If you find your thoughts returning to dark places, review these pages.

- Your mind is where greatness begins. A positive thinker has no limitations – because failure does not exist when you don't give up.

- When you think positively about something, you anticipate the successful outcome of that endeavor. Anticipation often leads to success.

- Plant the seeds of success in your life. Earning money is like being given a seed. You can give that seed away, to get something – or you can plant it. When you plant the seed, it grows into a tree that bears fruit. You need to save or invest your money instead of giving it to creditors so that it can grow and produce wealth.

- Commercial ads lead you off your destined path. They urge you to buy, stimulating your 'want' reflex. You've seen so many of these ads, 'want' has become more powerful than 'need.' Ignore these messages. They were created to fuel the cycle of debt.

- Being in debt lowers your standard of living. You might think you are 'keeping up with the Joneses,' but you are only making life difficult for yourself.

- Free yourself from debt, so that you can enjoy a positive mindset. Scale down, and start saving. Who cares what people will think! In the end, you will be wealthier and happier.

- Do not wear yourself out trying to be rich. Wealth comes and goes, but friends and family are forever. Remember your giving heart and what really matters on this earth.

- Ignore societal beliefs that make you feel inadequate and hopeless. Embrace the positive mindset, and enjoy a life of no limitations and endless opportunities.

- Use verbal affirmations internally and aloud. Create powerful, motivating affirmations that you can repeat to yourself to change your negative mindset into a positive one.

- Surround yourself with positive vibes! When you are positive about setbacks, the people around you will be too. Maintain an up-tempo, inspiring attitude for people to emulate.

- Be grateful for the things you have. Do not forget to thank God for what you do have, and take some time to think about the thousands of others who are less fortunate.

- Motivate yourself to succeed. When you feel yourself losing energy or consumed by fear or worry – give the worry to God, and push on. You need to get it done, and there is no point worrying about it now.

- The way you choose to see life is the way that you will experience it. Adopt a positive perspective so that you can be happier, stronger and full of hope.

CHAPTER FIVE

THE WISDOM OF GIVING

> *Everybody can be great... because anybody can serve. You don't have to have a college degree to serve. You don't have to make your subject and verb agree to serve. You only need a heart full of grace. A soul generated by love.*
>
> *– Martin Luther King, Jr.*

Giving Leads To Receiving

When a rich man gives money to help people in need, they are considered philanthropists. When a poor man gives his time to serve people in need – he is considered a hero. Giving is one of the most desirable traits anyone can possess. In these modern times, people believe that you can only give when you have money, or when you're in the financial position to give. But this is false.

There is so much more to giving than handing money over to someone that needs it. In our daily lives, we're confronted with people that need help. A selfless heart recognizes this need, and looks for a way to help. A selfish heart ignores the need, because it doesn't affect them in any way. God teaches us to help each other, however, and whenever we can.

This could mean seeing potential in an employee, and paying for them to take night classes. It could mean sharing food with strangers. It could even mean making the time to help your child with their homework. Every time you give, God blesses you. It's the giving and receiving principle, that has come to be known as 'karma' in the mainstream world. When you take the time to help others, they will have time to help you one day, when you need them.

This simple principle is a powerhouse in the business world. During your career, you'll meet many people that need help – and will be faced with a choice. Do you help them? Or do you ignore it? Ancient wisdom says, to give your time, your money and your life – for the enduring comfort of others in need. But giving doesn't only apply to charity, it applies to so many aspects of our lives.

Give your clients the best possible service, and you will be rewarded with long-term clients. Give your employees assistance and fair working conditions, and they'll work for you for years. The giving principle allows us to behave selflessly, for the benefit of those around us. The best part is that when you give freely, you achieve a sense of fulfillment that motivates and inspires you to do great things.

There's an ancient parable about the merits of giving. A wise woman was once traveling through a mountain pass, and came across a bubbling stream next to the roadside.

She noticed something glinting brighter than the clear water, and knelt down to pick it up. It was a precious stone, more beautiful than any she had ever seen. The following day, she came across a traveler who was wary and hungry. She opened her bag, and shared her food with him.

The tired traveler noticed the exquisite gem, and asked the women to give it to him as a gift. The wise women did so instantly, without hesitation. Later the traveler left, rejoicing in his good fortune. He knew the gem was enough to keep him fed and clothed for the rest of his life.

A few days later, the traveler returned – in a hurry to find the wise women that had given him the stone. "I've been thinking" he said to her, "I know how valuable this stone is, but I'm returning it to you in the hope that you'll give me something more valuable. Give me what you have within you, that allowed you to give me this stone."

In this parable, this traveler comes to understand the enduring power of selfless giving. We should all learn to give without hesitation – to anyone we can help. The more time and money we can give away – the better off we will be in our lives. Giving to others is immensely rewarding, and it liberates your soul.

Giving Leads to Abundance

When you give beyond all expectation, you will be blessed – by the Lord, and by the people around you. If all you can manage is time, or money, then invest it in people that need hope. You don't have to drop everything and volunteer at the local shelter, you can find ways in your own life to give. And there's a psychological factor that comes into play, while you're giving.

It's called the abundance mindset. When you give someone money that they need more than you do, you are creating an environment of abundance. This means that even if you can't afford to give, you are confident in the fact that more money will come in, and it won't be a problem. Money, in other words, will be in abundance. This will affect the way you do business, and how you conduct yourself.

Your behavior will change, based on the ancient principle of abundance. People have often found that when they give money, they receive a lot more in return. Whether it's the positive energy that you put out into the world after giving, that does this, or purely that 'karma' that happens when you're kind to people – it works. You should be a giving leader, in every sense of the word.

The Pathway To Innovation

We live in this massive information age. In America, even the working poor will never see anything near poverty, as it relates to other countries in the world. We have iPods, microwaves, and most American families have two cars. More than ever, there seems to be a sense that this is just the way it has always been, and I think this really hurts our ability to dream.

Dreaming and use of our imagination can atrophy, from lack of use, much like any of the other systems in the human body. As humans today, we don't feel the need to pursue these dreams, like those from our past.

What is there to achieve? We have concierge services, convenience stores, and the world at our fingertips. We have arrived! But this hasn't always been so. Pioneers came to America and had no choice but to dream.

If they wanted a better network of roads, it was a dream. If they wanted to create mass transit of goods, for their commerce to expand, they had to exploit the rivers for such demands.

Now more than ever, as you decide that you will dream, you will be a leader of epic proportions. In the twenty-first century, we label them innovators. Innovators by my definition, are leaders who solve problems very proactively and in many cases before anyone knows there's a problem!

This is happening in revolutionary ways, and those that do are multi millionaires and even billionaires in record time. Steve Jobs of Apple fame for example, decided that computers needed different typefaces or fonts. So, in 1984, he released the first computer that ever had different font styles – 12 to be exact.

A few years later, and TrueType was created – corrected the original blocky effect you'd get if you'd make your fonts very large. This resulted in global communities of designers coming up with new fonts that people could use for free. Who would have even thought that font choice would matter? Steve Jobs did, and he innovated.

He knew that this would be of importance and as an innovator, he solved this problem even before there was a noticeable void in the market. Look at the pride taken in the simple things! An innovator looks at the most minute details that make the difference. Look at the packaging used by Apple.

You can go on eBay and find boxes that sell for anywhere from $10 to $20 and it's just a container! Why? Because an innovator decided that the package itself should inspire. An innovator wants to make an impact. They want to serve. An innovator, at heart is an innate giver. They use their magical innovator abilities to give new and exciting things to the world. That's what you should be trying to do on a daily basis.

Innovation and a Giving Heart

The Biblical principle for the innovator was there long before the creators of Apple. The Bible says "Give and it shall be given." The innovator looks for ways to have an impact and serves the world. Man's laws can be avoided, sometimes for centuries, but Divine laws, can never be avoided. When tested, their resulting impact on your life WILL always be a response to the effort, or lack of some, in your life.

These basic laws are what guided the most successful men, before the history of our world was even chronicled, and they are still in place today. I have had the good fortune at a young age - to meet many innovators, and resulting millionaires. These men and women have been the recipients of Divine laws and most of them know the specific laws that are in place, and utilize them to their advantage.

According to these reverent ancient laws, selfishness will actually cause you to be poorer. This law says -"GIVE", and truthfully, I know selfish people that rarely find it easy to give in the first place. The behavior doesn't match this law. An innovator, by sheer nature of the process itself, must be 'the biggest' giver, but will have their own needs met in accordance with the law.

I will add, that there is a more amazing fact about this particular law in "Give and it shall be given." You don't receive what you give in equal measure, you actually receive considerably more in return. Give 2 and you get 3 back. Give 6 and you get 10, so to speak. In the Bible, there is a parable in Matthew 25, that says it best.

The Parable of The Ten Talents

Again, it will be like a man going on a journey, who called his servants and entrusted his property to them. To one he gave five talents of money, to another two talents, and to another one talent, each according to his ability.

Then he went on his journey. The man who had received the five talents went at once and put his money to work and gained five more. So also, the one with the two talents gained two more. But the man who had received the one talent went off, dug a hole in the ground and hid his master's money.

After a long time, the master of those servants returned and settled accounts with them. The man who had received the five talents brought the other five. "Master," he said, "you entrusted me with five talents. See, I have gained five more."

His master replied, "Well done, good and faithful servant! You have been faithful with a few things; I will put you in charge of many things. Come and share your master's happiness!" The man with the two talents also came. "Master," he said, "you entrusted me with two talents; see, I have gained two more."

His master replied, "Well done, good and faithful servant! You have been faithful with a few things; I will put you in charge of many things. Come and share your master's happiness!"

Then the man who had received the one talent came. "Master," he said, "I knew that you are a hard man, harvesting where you have not sown and gathering where you have not scattered seed. So, I was afraid and went out and hid your talent in the ground. See, here is what belongs to you."

His master replied, "You wicked, lazy servant! So you knew that I harvest where I have not sown and gather where I have not scattered seed? Well then, you should have put my money on deposit with the bankers, so that when I returned I would have received it back with interest.

"Take the talent from him and give it to the one who has the ten talents. For everyone who has will be given more, and he will have an abundance. Whoever does not have, even what he has will be taken from him. And throw that worthless servant outside, into the darkness..."

The World We Live In

We live in a negative society. We use negative words in daily speech that we don't even notice – like the fact that we call the sides of the loaf of the bread ends. They're actually two beginning pieces. Or when we call tow trucks, wreckers. There are even more negative expressions to describe how disillusioned we are as a society –

- Money doesn't grow on trees
- You can't have your cake, and eat it too
- You can't have everything
- I'm set in my ways
- It's beyond my control
- What's in it for me?
- You can't teach an old dog, new tricks

[1]A recent study by noted linguist Robert Schrauf, found that we have way more negative words in our vocabulary than positive ones. His study concluded that 50% of his test group used negative terms to describe their feelings.

Innovation in your home, business, job or industry, requires you to think about others. It requires you to help society get a better product or lifestyle. It requires you to think about your team, or those under you in your business or job. Our world is SO negative that we are brainwashed into worrying about ourselves, and it really does perpetuate negative thoughts.

We feel, "I want this", which results in selfish behavior – "I want to drive in this lane without you in front of me going 25 mph," We feel like if we have the things we want, we'll be happy, but that isn't true! This is something that the majority of us have to work on, and until we do, we will not see innovation.

If we don't see innovation, then in the end, we will not get what we ourselves really want. Pleasure seeking and a whole host

1 Schrauf, Robert. "Study: Negative Words Dominate Language" (Feb 2, 2005) ABC News http:// abcnews.go.com/Technology/DyeHard/story?id=460987&page=1#.TtzFRmOsARo

of moral degradation is an additional cause, and distracts us from others, and our ability to innovate and give.

How many super star athletes, or people who had incredible reach and influence - became tangled up in distractions related to moral degradation? Tiger Woods is a great example here.

There are sad stories like this, people who had amazing reach, and the potential to do exceptional things with it – but didn't, because the pursuit of pleasure permeated their entire life. The impact of a split second decision can remove Kings and Presidents from power, it can humble world class athletes, and paralyze your ability to impact the world.

Remember, that true success is not about pursuit of success, but victories. Victories in all aspects of our lives. Pleasure seeking MUST be managed with great vigilance, in order for you to achieve the greatest life that your Creator has mapped out for you. The key, is to think of others, and not yourself. To strive to help other people, instead of fulfilling your own selfish desires.

Innovation is not all roses. Eventual success is ALWAYS marred by a road of bad turns and negative breaks. But those who persist, will have won. Helen Keller said, *"The only thing worse than being blind, is having sight with no vision."*

Another innovator in history was Ludwig van Beethoven, who went deaf in his twenties, a horrible circumstance for a composer. He said, *"Then let us all do what is right, strive with all our might toward the unattainable, develop as fully as we can the gifts God has given us, and never stop learning."*

Even though he couldn't hear his own music, he continued to produce the world's most beautiful compositions, because he understood his art was for people, not himself.

These people's names are going to be locked into history, because they dreamed huge, and allowed those dreams to create burning desire - which in turn provided for immeasurable innovation. The gifts of their creation will go on forever.

Service, Desire and Success

When you are mindful of others in your daily life, it leads to increased success over time. This is because you foster a genuine desire to serve, which is applicable and advantageous at all levels of any career. The most giving innovators were obsessed with what they could do for the world, and how they could apply their talents to improve it for everyone.

This is the most noble goal a person can have, and one that often leads to fortune. You need to develop a giving heart, so that your hopes and dreams can take flight. God tells us in the Bible that the attitudes of our hearts are an important factor as to whether we receive, from the act of giving.

Giving to receive is not the right attitude. You must learn to give whole-heartedly, and happily – so that you can enjoy a bountiful life of abundance. Ancient wisdom says, you reap what you sow. That means when you give, you will be given, when you take, things will be taken from you. It's an old belief that holds true to this day.

It links back to the lesson that Jesus tries to teach us in Matthew 6: 19-21 –

"Do not store up for yourselves treasures on earth, where moth and rust destroy, and where thieves break in and steal. But store up for yourselves treasures in heaven, where moth and rust do not destroy, and where thieves do not break in and steal. For where your treasure is, there your heart will be also."

This ancient wisdom tells us that while it's alright to accumulate wealth on earth, this wealth is temporary, and doesn't have any real purpose after death. The only treasures we'll be able to take with us, are the ones we perform on earth – acts of love, charity and giving. These will be worth more in heaven than we could ever imagine.

Search your heart. If you've been giving tithes at church to impress other people, or to feel good about yourself – then you aren't giving with a pure heart. To give with a pure heart, you must do it for the right reasons. Give to help people. That means if someone needs your help, you have time for them. Whether it's a stranger, your spouse, child or distant cousin.

The way we serve other people, is directly related to our future success. The more you give, the more you'll receive. And each time you receive, you should give more – because that is the true heart of a giver. There is no expiry date for being kind and giving. When you receive, you can praise God by helping others – one of his divine laws that will continue to bless you in business.

It sounds like paradise, yes. But it can be a difficult habit to break. We are brought up to be selfish – "No one looks out for you, but you." So when it comes to giving, we can be reluctant about it, or suspicious of the people we're trying to help. A beggar on the side of the road might need food, but ask for change. Your immediate reaction is, if you give him money, he'll do something self-destructive with it.

We do live in a negative world, but one person can make a difference. Find ways around your negativity – buy the beggar a pie, instead of giving him change! There are so many people in the world that need help, and not just those less fortunate.

I've seen extremely wealthy men bow to depression, unable to pull themselves out from a crushing defeat. Be there when they need you. As time goes on, you will be able to give more because of God's grace!

The Amplification of Giving

Now that you've learned how important giving is to your life, you'll want to remember these special points.

- Nurture a selfless heart that looks for ways to help people in need.

- Be like the wise women, who gave away a priceless gem, and gained a life-long friend.

- Acknowledge the principle of abundance. When you believe that there is money in abundance, it will affect your behavior. Give freely and often, and have faith that God will provide you with whatever you need.

- Innovation is directly connected to the act of giving. Innovators spend their entire lives achieving, because of the belief that they have been charged with giving the world something special.

- Give and it shall be given. God promises that when you live with a giving heart, you will never be without.

- Remember the parable of the ten talents. When God blesses you with abilities, it is your responsibility to use them to help people. If you ignore them, or bury them in the sand like in the story – you will not receive in abundance. The more you give to the world, the more you'll get from it.

- Ignore the negativity that permeates our modern society. Stop being selfish in your actions.

- The only way to prevent instant gratification that sometimes becomes moral decay, is to put others before yourself.

- Give with a pure heart, don't give to receive.

- Acknowledge the people in your life, and care for them. Give openly and honestly, and do your best to serve with a giving heart.

CHAPTER SIX

THE WISDOM OF SELF-DISCIPLINE

> *Control is not leadership; management is not leadership; leadership is leadership is leadership. If you seek to lead, invest at least 50% of your time leading yourself—your own purpose, ethics, principles, motivation, conduct. Invest at least 20% leading those with authority over you and 15% leading your peers. If you don't understand that you work for your mislabeled 'subordinates,' then you know nothing of leadership. You know only tyranny.*
>
> **– Dee Hock, Founder Emeritus, VISA International**

Control and The Passive Mindset

> *A person without self-control is as defenseless as a city with broken down walls*
>
> Proverbs 24-28.

This is a very powerful element of life that will stop you from being massively successful, quicker than most anything.

Successful people are successful because they do the very things that unsuccessful people don't like to do! The amazing thing is, that successful people do them and do them relentlessly, because they know that they will achieve the success that they desire.

Get this – if you can get yourself to do what you MUST do to ensure your success, no matter the cost, considering this is on a moral base, then your success is virtually guaranteed. Ancient wisdom says that self-control is your greatest ally in the war against procrastination. What sells me on doing the hard things on a daily basis, is that 'virtually guaranteed' part. This law is a fundamental principle that secures your success!

I have a friend of mine that puts a frog on his desk. He uses the frog as a comparison to those activities that repel him the most. At the end of the day, he knows the work will pay him in 'green.' Every day when he gets to work, he doesn't do anything other than his dollar producing activities - and that frog stays front and center, to remind him of what he needs to do. Once he is done, he can put the frog away until the next morning. Maybe you need a frog in your life?

How many of us can say we are truly in control of what we do every day? Very few! Sometimes we float through our days, doing very little. You're not crushing it! Or worse, you're working yourself to death and not seeing any results. What's going on? You need to learn about active and passive mindsets.

The Active and Passive Minds

The passive mindset is, unfortunately, the mindset we're taught to adopt from a very young age. We are seated in front of the television and computer, as passive viewers, and information comes to us. We are watching others do and live their lives. The passive mindset is the ultimate 'spectator to life'

But this isn't how business works. You can do 'everything' right in business, and still not achieve much. It's because you are applying a passive mindset to your work.

A passive mind waits around for things to happen. It puts in some work, and then waits for miracles to happen. James for example, runs his own IT firm. He did everything that his friend George did, but George was much more successful. Why? They both set up websites. They both ran ad campaigns. They both did great work for their clients. Then, one day they had a conversation about it.

Turns out, they weren't doing the same things at all. James launched his website, and just left it there – for 2 years. George on the other hand, continually tweaked it, improved its search rankings and updated it often. James ran the same ads every month, while George split tested ads to find which ones yielded higher returns. They both did great work, but George kept in touch with his old clients by asking them to join an email list – which then got him repeat business.

James was passive in his business process, while George was active. The big difference? The active mind constantly seeks out new knowledge, and attempts to apply that knowledge to the real world. The passive mind doesn't do that. Most of us are stuck in a passive mindset. The world goes by, and we don't feel very empowered to make things happen. Even if we have good ideas, they seem too hard, and there's just no time to make them happen.

Remember the negative mindset we spoke about earlier?

A negative mind is a passive mind, and a passive mind has no control. You want to change your mindset to an active one, so that you can begin asserting yourself, controlling your environment and making things happen. An active mindset oozes control and discipline. It thrives on getting things done, because it is constantly thinking. The mind works because you are constantly learning, and looking for new ways to make things work.

It all feeds into each other. To become a master of self-control, you must first force yourself to break old, terribly destructive habits. These changes will form the foundation of your new active mindset.

The Power of Positive Habits

You might need a frog like that friend of mine. Something to keep reminding you that your goals exist and that each day counts towards them. A self-disciplined person is a person of positive habits. You need these habits to keep you on the straight and narrow, working towards your goals.

"Motivation is what gets you started. Habit is what keeps you going."

Isolate the big things in your life that you need to get done. Then refine these goals into daily tasks. What makes bank? Is it your goal to improve your cash flow? What do you need to do to make that happen? A calendar is a useful tool in the battle of the wills. It behaves as a reward system, when you get to cross off the date, and know that you've done well that day.

If you need to sit down in the morning and contact all of your clients, then do it. If it helps, see it as a structural game.

Every time you finish a call, reward yourself with something. The trick is to make this new process a daily habit. A desirable habit, one that could change the way you do business.

Do not set some mystical future time, start now. It takes a month to form a habit, and once you're into it, it will seem like second nature. Push through and make it work. Even if the job is terrible, just get it done! Do it! Do not do tomorrow, what you can do right now! Procrastination is the enemy of positive habits and self-discipline.

Mastering Your Actions, Will and Drive

"The secret of success is learning how to use pain and pleasure instead of having pain and pleasure use you. If

you do that, you're in control of your life. If you don't, life controls you."

- Anthony Robbins

It's funny how when we really don't want to do something, we find a million other things to do. In real life, this sets us back and wastes our time – two things you will never find a self-disciplined person doing. When you become self disciplined, you learn to master your actions, your will and your drive.

It begins backwards with the drive to do something. This drive gives you the willpower to sit down and take action. It's a proven scientific fact that people with greater self-control go on to lead greater lives – with more success financially and personally. These people are naturally strong willed, and are able to deny themselves anything to achieve a greater goal.

That's what you need to become - *iron willed*. Because of the instant gratification we are used to as society, our wills have become weak. If we don't want to do something enough, we just don't do it. And the world tells us it's okay, as long as it makes us happy. The thing is – instant gratification never makes us happy for very long. Every day in our lives is a test of will.

You make decisions according to your wants and desires – not your needs. Now, you need to start thinking of these needs. You need to achieve this goal. Or more to the point, you NEED to get that piece of work done every day to achieve the desired result. The only thing holding you back is your weak will and talent for procrastination. It wears people away, and steals their dreams.

There are many reasons why many people have weak wills. Mostly it is because of that sense of 'entitlement' that comes from working hard. It's another reason why letting yourself rest and recuperate on weekends, is so important. It recharges your willpower! There was a study that placed people in two separate rooms. They were told not to eat the night before. Each room contained a delicious plate of frosted cupcakes, a plate of hard radishes – and a puzzle.

Half the test subjects were told to eat the radishes, but not touch the delicious cupcakes. The other half was told to eat the yummy cupcakes and not the radishes. Then they all did the puzzle. The trick of course, was that the puzzle was unsolvable. It was a test of wills, to see if people who were allowed the delicious cupcakes would do better than the slighted radish-eaters.

And you know what? All of the radish eaters gave up on their puzzles before the cupcake eaters did. It proves that willpower is not unlimited. The radish eaters already exercised willpower by not eating the cupcakes. They had a little leftover to use on the puzzle, but gave up as they ran out. Many tests have been conducted along these lines – all with the same result.

That's why mastering your willpower means you need to be focused, disciplined and prepared for the task at hand. You can't be exhausted, frustrated or overworked – or you'll never see it through. That's how you master your actions, will and drive. By working hard when you have to, and resting when you need to. Not working hard when it suits you, and resting when you feel like it.

How To Get The Most Out of Willpower

You might be thinking, 'So how do I learn how to strengthen my will?' A good start is by forming habits, because it effectively increases your willpower tolerance level. In other words, the more you practice having willpower, the more you will have. Think of it like a muscle that needs to be exercised. Force yourself to do those little important things you hate doing, and soon they won't even bother you anymore.

We are all slaves to our impulses. Strengthening your willpower helps you overcome these impulses – or more directly, teaches you to control them. You can then decide whether you do or don't want to do something. Restricting your behavior teaches you how to master your emotions. Instead of being ruled by them, you rule them.

You can then put them to work, towards your eventual success. Imagine if every ounce of your talent and ability was channeled into the right areas every day! It would change your life, nearly overnight! No more laziness or procrastination, just pure self-discipline and all the rewards that come with it.

Never allow your laziness to overcome you, to the point where it forces you to do nothing, when you should be doing something important. There's nothing relaxing about putting things off – so you might as well do them now, with a smile on your face! If you haven't already figured it out, life is a constant test of wills.

You do certain things in your life – right? But, there are things you'd never do. This is where your willpower draws the line. Even if you want to do something – it's too bad for you. And now, you don't really think about it, because it's a natural response. You need to get yourself to the point where working hard and smart for your goals is a natural response. You want to do it. You need to do it! There's no room for laziness!

It is NOT about what you want to do anymore.

It is about what you NEED to do.

You have to deny your lazy impulses and pull through. You don't deserve to just lie there and sleep, when you should be working. You aren't entitled to take an extra break because you've been working hard. This is your life. Your future. When you procrastinate it stifles your dreams, not someone else's.

Many experts have pointed out that a lack of self-discipline could be one of the reasons why so many Americans are out of work these days, or struggle with debt. When you live with debt, it takes enormous willpower to break that cycle. To get out from under the collective creditor hive. But once you do, you will see greater rewards than ever before.

Ancient wisdom says that the best rewards are the ones that take extreme self-discipline. Without it, you can't be great. Without it, you can't thrive – no matter how big your dreams are. Self-discipline allows you to put those goals into action, and keeps you working at them until you're successful.

Look at the greatest people of our time – they didn't stop until they reached their goals. Then they set new ones, and followed different paths. That's what you need to learn to do, before you can finally be successful.

The Elixir of Success

Exhibiting self-control in all things is key. This is the elixir to massive success. It's inside nearly every massively successful person, in the world. Success is momentum based. One success breeds another, and another success breeds another, and the pace increases. Just the same, every act of self-control causes you to love and respect yourself even more.

Your self-esteem goes up, and this affects the power of your perception. People around you see you differently, those that need to bend to your leadership will, and the businesses you want to work with will notice you.

Keeping with that momentum - imagine the credibility you'll have, because you are self-disciplined. One of my favorite daily affirmations is this – *"Do what you know you must do to be successful, and your success is virtually guaranteed."*

This helps me take on the challenging, but dollar producing part of my day. It makes me want to think big. Being a real estate consultant, you might be inclined to start your day with an 'easier' or smaller client. When I think of this affirmation, it changes my framework. I want to come in like a gangbuster. My thoughts shift from looking for the easy, low hanging fruit - to thinking 'Big Deals pay Big Money.'

I am super focused in the mornings. My days before noon, are centered around doing huge things that I would usually shy away from. These produce very large goals or reach in the business. You can do this too, by forming habits, and focusing on delivering self-discipline and self-control in all that you do.

I have a friend Bill, who owns a national firm that sells services business to business. This man's company is probably in the $20 to $30 million a year range. We were talking one day about pushing our businesses to the next level. He told me that he was really into numbers, and that his controller quit - so he was going to manage the books himself for his firm. This absolutely blew my mind, and I called him out on it, in love of course.

Bill did not get into business-to-business sales on a national level, by managing the books for the business. He didn't get there by answering all of the phone calls. He didn't get there by making sure the toilets were clean. He got there by being a good CEO, and a hard businessman, to get to where he is today.

I said "Bill, why are you avoiding what you should be doing at work every day? Have you suddenly developed an aversion to being in charge? Being the lead sales person for your company?" He was stunned, but he knew I was right.

The amazing thing is, that you can go to your business every flipping day, and do a whole bunch of busy-ness but not do 5 whole minutes of business. We've all done it, many don't even realize that we're doing it!

Separate Busy-ness From Business

The higher the value of your task, the more money you are making - and the more profitable you become. But we can become so delirious as to what we should be doing, that we don't do anything.

Instead, we find ourselves frittering our days away, doing nothing of high value, and then coming home, sitting in our easy chair feeling like we did something amazing today.

On the other hand, sometimes your subconscious is yelling at you saying "Get to the hard things, and give yourself a RAISE!" We are smart humans though, and we know how to turn the volume down on that little voice don't we? Shame on us. The value of a day given to the highest possible tasks, is a day where the rewards are heaped on us with the knowledge, that we really lived as our best selves.

Nothing feels better. And remember, separate busy-ness from business. There is no shortage of time, only a shortage of direction. Write that down. It's not a time thing, it's a 'focus-on-the-wrong-thang' thing.

Starve that part of you that wants you to live below your own standards. Focus only on what really matters – find your zone, and you will be amazed at how the day looks. Grasping this alone, would have an amazing impact on you.

The world is teeming with brands that try and sell you quick fix solutions, or get rich quick schemes. The reality is that their solutions don't exist. They are not a substitute for willpower. And that's exactly what they try to tell you. You don't have to be determined or have self-control, you just need product x!

Using Self-Discipline Correctly

You can't be super motivated and charged with self-discipline all of the time. That's why you have to learn to apply it to the part of your day that matters most. If you have a particularly challenging project and you're dreading it – then you know that's where you need to focus your attention. In fact, as soon as you feel the desire to not do it, you should dive in and get it done!

The sooner you complete it, the quicker it will be behind you. And best of all, you'll have done it in record time, and can reap the financial rewards. No more putting it off, day after day – until the last minute. Because when you do that – the busy-ness creeps in, and you don't do any significant work. Your mind knows it's avoiding something, so it decides to do silly things that don't really matter.

You can apply self-discipline to any aspect of your life, but it will make the most impact for you in business. Do you know what great work ethic looks like? It is not someone that pretends to work hard, it's someone that gets the important things done quickly, so that they can focus their energies on other things.

Self-discipline becomes an immaculate work ethic. When you own and run your own business, you can take this trait all the way to the bank.

Ancient wisdom says, that to see massive accomplishments in life, you must be self-disciplined. Believe in your abilities and overcome those challenges and terrible traits that tend to make you laid back.

You can and will be better. All it takes is exercising your willpower, some motivation – and an aggressive plan of attack! I like to remind myself to 'crush it' before I do something I'd rather not do. It gives me energy, and challenges me to be my best. You need to crush it more often, so that you achieve your desired goals.

The Amplification of Self-Discipline

You're ready to take on the world. But you need to review the finer details of how exactly you can 'crush it' on a daily basis.

- A person without self-control is like a city with broken down walls. Anything can get in, even if you don't want it too.

- If you can get yourself to do what you MUST do to ensure your success, no matter the cost, then your success is virtually guaranteed.

- Change from a passive to an active mindset. Learn more, do more and apply more knowledge in the real world than you ever have before.

- The active mind constantly seeks out new knowledge, and attempts to apply that knowledge to the real world. The passive mind doesn't do that.

- To become a master of self-control, you must first force yourself to break old, terribly destructive habits. These habits will form the foundation of your new active mindset.

- Remember - "Motivation is what gets you started. Habit is what keeps you going."

- Don't set some mystical future time, start now. It takes a month to form a habit, and once you're into it, it will seem like second nature. Push through and make it work. Even if the job is terrible, just get it done! Do it! Don't do tomorrow, what you can do right now! Procrastination is the *enemy* of positive habits and self-discipline.

- We are all slaves to our impulses. Strengthening your willpower helps you overcome these impulses – or more directly, teaches you to control them.

- Never allow your laziness to overcome you, to the point where it forces you to do nothing, when you should be doing something important. Ancient wisdom says that the best rewards are the ones that take extreme self-discipline.

- Success is momentum based. One success breeds another, and another success breeds another, and the pace increases. Just the same, every act of self-control causes you to love and respect yourself even more.

- Self-discipline becomes an immaculate work ethic. When you own and run your own business, you can take this trait all the way to the bank. Ancient wisdom says, that to work hard you must be self-disciplined. Believe in your abilities and overcome those challenges and terrible traits that tend to make you laid back.

CHAPTER SEVEN

THE WISDOM OF THINKING BIG

> *Imagination is more important than knowledge. For knowledge is limited to all we now know and understand, while imagination embraces the entire world, and all there ever will be to know and understand.*
> *– Albert Einstein*

Repression and Untapped Talent

Each one of us is born with strengths and talents, and the potential to do great things with these gifts. So, why do so many people never achieve their true potential? Once again, we zoom in, on the heart of modern day society. Psychological repression occurs when you repel your desires, impulses and instincts, and keep them subdued in the subconscious.

We've already learned that desire is a key motivator in the quest to attain victories in life. When you have grown up with a narrow view of life, believing that nothing is possible – you tend to repress any 'big thinking' and shy away from exercising your God given imagination. When you're unable to release that side of yourself that can dream beyond your circumstances, and I mean dream big – then you are able to challenge yourself and access your untapped talent.

Imagine if everything you thought you could do, or be – could happen. The greatest men and women in history have often regarded unrealistic plans and dreams as the benchmark of greatness. I believe we understand ourselves much more than we are allowed to acknowledge as people.

We know that we can achieve exceptional things. But because the people around us are bogged down with daily life, and are disillusioned by their circumstances – they are unable to support these big dreams. Instead they'll laugh, or tell you it's impossible. Without support or validation, it can be extremely difficult to push forward with your dreams.

It's natural to want to feel like you are working towards something tangible, and that comes from the validation you get from others. The only problem? True greatness is really a solitary act. Knowing that deep down you have untapped potential that could change your life, is something only you can truly understand.

It's a feeling that can't be communicated to someone else. Dreams and imagination fuel desire, spark focus and force you to pursue that definitive end goal. Without a dream, the most talented man on earth would amount to nothing more than the mediocre minds around him.

But you're not the sum of collective self-worth. Ancient wisdom says that thinking big is the mark of a person heading towards success. We're taught to set small, realistic goals – but to disregard those flamboyant, ambitious dreams of the impossible. Why?

If you can't dream it, you can't do it! Repression of desire squanders your natural talent. When you don't have something huge to work towards, you'll never be able to push yourself, and discover a whole new level potential that you didn't even realize you had before. Remember you have to 'crush it!'

Unlocking the Talent Inside You

Many people wander through life without a purpose, a mission to fuel their success. This is because your imagination is not working hard enough, to secure those dreams in your mind. There are several lessons to be learned about thinking big and unlocking the talent within you. Right now, you are trapped in bad habits that limit your mindset, potential and capacity to excel.

The first thing you need to do is acknowledge that you are an individual, and that the people around you are also individuals. Each of you have inner strength and are powerful – because of your ability to dream big. Using your imagination means creating a connection between your future and your present.

It increases your timeline, and your thought progression, so that you're constantly working towards an attainable ideal. This means your short-term goals will become more streamlined, and will support your long-term goals as well.

You see, our lives revolve around the amount of effort we put into things every day. When you go to work, you exert a certain amount of effort. When you make dinner, you put a certain amount of effort into the food. Above all, dreams help you put in the maximum amount of effort, in the shortest amount of time.

Because you have your end goal firmly in place, you are able to work towards it with speed and vigor, using every ounce of your untapped talent. Ancient wisdom has always said that what you put in, is what you'll get out. Using your imagination drives you towards that goal, and forces you to utilize your talents in new and exciting ways.

Effort is also directly connected to action. You've built up a lifetime's supply of knowledge, and have never used it properly. Even Einstein said that imagination is more important than knowledge. This is because without imagination, you are unable to efficiently use the knowledge you've accumulated, towards a positive goal.

Controlling Your Imagination

You were born with the ability to use 'inner vision' or imagination, without even knowing it. Every day, your imagination runs wild, allowing certain ideas and thoughts into your head – whether they be positive or negative. That's the exceptional thing about thinking big. You channel your energy into using your imagination to manifest positive visions, that reinforce your goals. Remember when I said most people need support and validation? This is one way you can support yourself.

Seeing mental images of future circumstances or events, can be harnessed. It empowers you to believe that this future will happen, as you become more and more familiar with it.

The whole 'fake it, until you make it' concept comes from using your imagination to positively re-enforce your actions. When you believe that you are already something – because your dreams have made it real in your mind – that's when achievement is just around the corner.

You can learn to control your imagination. Reject all negative visions of your future, and replace them with big dreams. If that means closing your eyes before you go to sleep every night, and actively imagining yourself in that position – then that's something you should be doing. Great people do this naturally. Their dreams are so big, so all encompassing, that they work very hard to make them a reality.

The Laboratory of The Mind

We live in a negative world, so much so, that we don't focus ourselves towards things that will ultimately change our lives, and the world. I believe that you can create anything that you can imagine. In every generation, the world is enhanced by a handful of remarkably imaginative people. And we were created, to be creators.

We were created with an amazing laboratory, a fertile ground, where anything you ever dreamed could be developed and executed to perfection. I'm not saying this to be nuanced, or freakishly positive. I'm convinced that our only real barriers, within reason, lie in our ability to develop and utilize our imaginations.

We lack freethinking and creativity, and I can't help but go back to our current approach to life. We just don't think big enough! For us to better understand imagination, it's imperative that we consider its two main parts.

Synthetic imagination is the basic form of thought that is fueled by past and present experiences. It's a view of the database of experiences one has already had. It's not generating any new concepts. This part of the imagination creates nothing new. An inventor or an engineer would work from this laboratory of thought, basically using trial and error as a guide.

Creative imagination on the other hand, is a premise where the mind pushes out ideas that are completely organic and free of fixed concepts - that were already in place in the mind. This faculty of thought is very intriguing. Science indicates that this thought process operates when the conscious mind is working at a very high pace.

The creative faculty also produces more when there is a strong desire in place to achieve something. Another important item to note, is that creative imagination works best through frequency and development. To that end, it resembles a muscle. The best writers, composers, marketers, leaders of business, finance and industry, are all world-class masters of the use of creative imagination.

Desire is nothing more than an internal emotion; it's powerless until it's deployed into physical action. While synthetic imagination is most used and available to us, the pursuit of the very best in life, will place us in circumstances where we will need to tap the power of creative imagination.

Give your imagination a workout. Desire can drive you to the material goal that you seek, the accomplishments that you aspire to. Imagination is the key to CONVERT the desire into, let's say money, as an example. Transforming the impulse of desire into tangible money will require a plan, and the plan itself must be derived from synthetic imagination.

Creative imagination allows us to see beyond the physical world, to become aware of things that could happen – if we allow them to. There has never been a highly successful person that achieved all they did without an incredible imagination. They dared to think big, not just once, but constantly.

It's imagination that takes a poor man and transforms him into someone with wealth. Not only thinking, but believing that these visualizations will manifest is key to attaining business success.

Divine Intelligence and Potential

It's highly recommended that you read through this book completely, and discover all of the collective knowledge here. Each piece of knowledge contained here will aid in your success - in transforming your plan into the receiving of your financial goal. The first thing you must do is to map your plan and write it down. Writing down your plan is key, and allows life to enter your very ideas.

It gives your ideas roots and is the concrete that holds the foundation of your ideas in place. Get clear on your desire, reduce it to a plan through synthetic imagination and put it in writing – these steps alone, will move you onto a pathway to success. The brain itself is made of millions of cells. This organ is a mass of energy. Desire is a thought impulse, that contains energy!

Your Creator armed you with an amazing arsenal to live an incredibly successful life. Our example is money – when you give desire 'life' through thought impulse, you are essentially drafting into your service, an amazing force which was shared by Divine Intelligence, to create this amazing world we share.

In the Bible, our Creator made us 'in His image.' The ability and power behind desire, was crafted and used by God himself for this statement to be true, and from the results, it clearly is. You can build a fortune, a life you have never dreamed, all by mastering and understanding this ancient wisdom.

And you may think that this must be some elaborate secret, but it really isn't. Nature itself is a banner of representation, proving that these laws are true. Take the story of Dr Frank Gunsaulus, an average man, a preacher – who needed a million dollars to make his dreams come true. Here is his story.

The Million Dollar Sermon

Dr. Gunsaulus was quite a forward thinking man, who dreamed of one day heading an educational institution, where he could teach his students to learn by doing. It was his deepest desire since his college days, where he noticed many defects in the current educational system – defects he knew he could fix.

Dr. Gunsaulus decided to organize a new college, based on these principles – that wouldn't be shackled by the older methods of teaching. The big problem? He needed a million dollars to do it. A millions dollars! Most of us would have given up – without any means of generating, earning or borrowing that kind of money.

The young preacher obsessed about where and how he would get his million dollars. He needed it, he wanted it – and he was going to get it. But how would he get this money that needed so desperately needed? He couldn't seem to figure it out. Every night he went to bed, obsessing about his million dollars. When he woke every morning, the first thought in his mind was about the money.

Everywhere he went, he obsessed about his million. The million that would allow him to establish his college. He understood that a million dollars was a lot of money – but he also understood that limitations are a construction of the mind. As a philosopher and preacher, Dr Gunsaulus recognized that definiteness of purpose is the starting point of all things. He also noticed that purpose takes on life and power when backed by burning desire. The intangible must become the material!

He understood all of these ancient truths, but still had no idea where he'd get his million dollars. If any of us were in that position, we would have moved on to something else. It's just too hard, and impossible. But that's not what he did. Here's exactly as he tells it.

[2]"One Saturday afternoon I sat in my room thinking of ways and means of raising the money to carry out my plans. For nearly two years, I had been thinking, but I had done nothing but think!

---

2 Hill, Napoleon. "Think and Grow Rich" Chapter 6: Imagination. http://www.sacred-texts.com/nth/tgr/tgr11.htm

The time had come for ACTION!

I made up my mind, then and there, that I would get the necessary million dollars within a week. How? I was not concerned about that. The main thing of importance was the decision to get the money within a specified time, and I want to tell you that the moment I reached a definite decision to get the money within a specified time, a strange feeling of assurance came over me, such as I had never before experienced.

Something inside me seemed to say, 'Why didn't you reach that decision a long time ago? The money was waiting for you all the time!' Things began to happen in a hurry. I called the newspapers and announced I would preach a sermon the following morning, entitled, 'What I would do if I had a Million Dollars.'

I went to work on the sermon immediately, but I must tell you, frankly, the task was not difficult, because I had been preparing that sermon for almost two years. The spirit back of it was a part of me! Long before midnight, I had finished writing the sermon. I went to bed and slept with a feeling of confidence, for I could see myself already in possession of the million dollars.

Next morning I arose early, went into the bathroom, read the sermon, then knelt on my knees and asked that my sermon might come to the attention of someone who would supply the needed money.

While I was praying, I again had that feeling of assurance that the money would be forthcoming. In my excitement, I walked out without my sermon, and did not discover the oversight until I was in my pulpit and about ready to begin delivering it.

It was too late to go back for my notes, and what a blessing that I couldn't go back! Instead, my own subconscious mind yielded the material I needed. When I arose to begin my sermon,

I closed my eyes, and spoke with all my heart and soul of my dreams. I not only talked to my audience, but I fancy I talked also to God.

I told what I would do with a million dollars if that amount were placed in my hands. I described the plan I had in mind for organizing a great educational institution, where young people would learn to do practical things, and at the same time develop their minds. When I had finished and sat down, a man slowly arose from his seat, about three rows from the rear, and made his way toward the pulpit.

I wondered what he was going to do. He came into the pulpit, extended his hand, and said, 'Reverend, I liked your sermon. I believe you can do everything you said you would, if you had a million dollars. To prove that I believe in you and your sermon, if you will come to my office tomorrow morning, I will give you the million dollars. My name is Phillip D. Armour."

Dr Gunsaulus was presented with a million dollars in Mr. Armour's office the next day. He used this money to found the Armour Institute of Technology. The preacher's idea was backed with burning desire. Once he had reached the decision to get it in his own mind, it took him 36 hours to make it happen!

This is the importance of planning when you come across an idea you'd like to see materialize. Ideas can't come to life, if there is no definitive purpose behind them. He decided he'd give himself one week to make it happen. His mind sprang into action, and he did in fact make big things come to life. He is living proof that ideas can be turned into cash through the power of definite purpose and definite plans.

There is unlimited power in clarity of vision and forced action. Visualizing a positive outcome and fervently believing it is the first step to something big. Add desire and that plan of action, and anything can happen.

If you are a person who believes that riches and success come by the basic tenants of hard work and honesty alone, you are far from accurate! Riches and success, when and if they come, will appear IN RESPONSE to a definite plan that was imposed on them, and in no way by chance or luck. Believe that. Your plan actually pursues that object you desire, and the object simply reacts to the pursuit!

An idea is a pulse of thought energy that causes action by appealing to the imagination. The best sales people I have been fortunate to know, are aware that an idea can be sold when the merchandise can't be. The 'regular' sales people don't know this, and this is why they are only 'average'.

Have you ever gone to a bookstore and reviewed the titles and covers of the books? Bookmakers are brilliant in that they know if the cover looks good, you just might pick it up - even if there is nothing in between the covers. You want big things to happen in your life? Then create an idea. Define a plan, and reduce it to writing.

The awesome thing is that you will give it life, you will nurture the idea, but over time, the idea will gradually start to almost execute the plan on its own. And as it materializes, it will even begin to actively sweep aside opposition. This is where the real excitement lies, in the creative imagination. The plan of action will attract what you seek.

Visualizing and Your Plan of Action

History has taught us that when you visualize something and come up with a plan to make this happen – even just a timeframe – then it can, and will happen. Most people fail because they never realize that this singular principle of ancient wisdom exists.

There is a break down between wanting something, and making it happen.

We become tormented by the 'fact' that we are powerless, when we're not! How can I take this HUGE idea and make it a reality? How can I get that amount of money? If you obsess about it long enough, that the idea becomes a burning desire, then your mind will naturally begin to toy with different plans. Eventually you will settle on a plan, and make it work.

For most of us, these plans might not pan out the first time. They might not even pan out several times in a row. That's where persistence comes in.

Determination and the will to continue reviewing and renewing your plan until it works. Each time you'll experience different results and will learn from them.

The key is to never give up. The right plan will always result in rewards.

The Amplification of Imagination

What key points can you take away from this chapter? Let's review.

- Don't repress or stifle your natural ability to dream, and use that God given imagination.

- The greatest men and women in history have often regarded unrealistic plans and dreams as the benchmark of greatness.

- You don't need validation from other people. Dreams and imagination fuel desire, spark focus and force you to pursue that definitive end goal. Without a dream, the most talented man on earth would amount to nothing more than the mediocre minds around him.

- Above all, dreams help you put in the maximum amount of effort, in the shortest amount of time.

- Without imagination, you are unable to efficiently use the knowledge you've accumulated, towards a positive goal.

- Our only real barriers, within reason, lie in our ability to develop and utilize our imaginations.

- Synthetic imagination is the basic form of thought, that is fueled by past and present experiences. It's a view of the database of experiences one has already had.

- Creative imagination is a premise where the mind pushes out ideas that are completely organic and free of fixed concepts - that were already in place in the mind.

- Desire is nothing more than an internal emotion; it's powerless until it's deployed into physical action.

- Writing down your plan is key, and allows life to enter your very ideas.

- Ideas can't come to life, if there is no definitive purpose behind them.

- There is unlimited power in clarity of vision and forced action. Visualizing a positive outcome and fervently believing it is the first step to something big. Add desire to that plan of action, and anything can happen.

- Have the determination and the will to continue reviewing and renewing your plan until it works. Each time you will experience different results and will learn from them.

CHAPTER EIGHT

THE WISDOM OF INNOVATION

Your time is limited, so don't waste it living someone else's life. Don't be trapped by dogma – which is living with the results of other people's thinking. Don't let the noise of others' opinions drown out your own inner voice. And most important, have the courage to follow your heart and intuition. They somehow already know what you truly want to become.

– Steve Jobs

Why Innovation is a Rarity

Innovation is rare. It's not about general knowledge but specialized knowledge. There are two main kinds of knowledge, specialized and general. There is an abundance of general knowledge in the world. Our universities are full of general knowledge – books are revised around the clock practically, yet professors, who give out this vast knowledge aren't themselves very wealthy.

Knowledge alone, can't give a benefit, but it's the organized and systematic fashion of disbursement of general knowledge – then called specialized knowledge, that causes abundance in that person who compiles it. Knowledge is powerless to attain money. There is the long-standing futile adage that says 'knowledge is power.'

Knowledge, in and of itself, is powerless. Only with organized knowledge can a superior service be rendered, and wealth itself be harnessed. The shame of our schools and colleges is the failure to not only drive students to collect general knowledge, but to sort and arrange it to inspire innovation.

The tech revolution has inspired a number of dropouts who then became billionaires, why? Because they had a ravenous appetite to arrange and organize general knowledge, the world was blessed with the likes of passionate innovations. Edison had 3 months of school his entire life, and his massive focus to arrange knowledge, brought the light that you are sitting under, as you likely read this.

Ford had less than a 10th grade education, and yet you possibly drove home today in one of his cars! You were most likely on an Apple or a Microsoft product in the last 24 hours, both from the likes of Bill Gates and Steve Jobs, who found college a bit off the mark from what they wanted.

Statistically, you have probably had exposure to Facebook as well, which means, another college dropout developed something (NOT BECAUSE he graduated with a masters) but because he took knowledge and organized it to change the world. It drives me crazy to hear people say, "I am going back for my 4th masters because I just can't get a foot hold in the market."

If I do that, then it will pay off. Yeah! Then you will have student loans for another 35 years! You might pay off your house sooner. Don't get me wrong, some of the best people I have ever worked with are incredibly sharp people, and it was a credit to their grasp of general knowledge through higher learning venues, but don't think for a moment that you have any hindrance on your life because you don't have some special job placement or under graduate's degree. That is bunk.

We are told repeatedly to get formal training, to learn, learn, learn! We must have massive volumes of general knowledge in order to succeed! This just isn't the case. Henry Ford had armies of men who worked for him. Countless improvements to the Ford car were only there because he 'knew' who 'knew!' That means, he didn't possess the knowledge directly, but he obtained the knowledge by use of the person who had expertise in a given area.

Understand, that money is made, that value is given in the organization because of the arrangement of knowledge, not because of the knowledge base. There are just certain things that you don't have to spend four years learning; there is a lot of knowledge that you need, but you don't need it all in your own mind!

The earning power comes by learning organization of that knowledge. Honestly, one of the smartest things that one can learn, is how to organize human capital. Look at the Steel Magnate - Carnegie. It was said at one time in the early 1900s, that he had 43 Millionaires working for him at once! This was back when a million bucks was a lot of money!

When asked how so many people could be worth so much at any one given time, Carnegie said, "You know when you go in to work with people, you look at it just like you do a gold mine – you expect to move a whole heck of a lot of dirt to get to the gold, but you aren't looking for the dirt."

He knew that organizing and leading men was actually organizing a large knowledge base. Leadership can be one of the most rewarding and highest paying jobs. CEOs and Presidents are to collect and organize ideas and knowledge from thousands of people under them, for the good of not only themselves, but the people under them.

We have become mind numbed on general education and have literally altered our true impact on the world from not exploiting our ability to organize, imagine, and think creatively. Evidence shows that this was a way of life for people – that there wasn't this long standing process to say, 'I am getting a diploma, so that I can work for someone else.'

We have literally boxed ourselves in – we are the proverbial 'nothing but a number,' to ourselves, and to the bosses in the world. While this emphasis hasn't been general knowledge focused, we are now there – it's this century, and I think our children and some generations ahead will face this. I want to make it clear, that the most amazing people in our current time get this, and exploit it to the maximum.

Pushing the creative faculties to the max, the spirit of opening our minds and imagination must be taught and channeled into our personal lives, as well as to our kids.

There is no price limit for sound ideas! If you have not landed your big idea, don't give up. The most powerful nation on earth isn't Russia, and it's not America, it's 'imagi-nation.'

Imagination is the key skill needed to pair up a good idea, with specialized knowledge, then there is no limit to what can happen. In fact, in history there have been a number of ideas that haven't changed the world, yet still made their innovators rich.

The inventor of OxiClean, took an active ingredient that anyone could have bought from a pool supply shop, and created this bestselling product. It was marketed as a miracle cleanser, because the ingredient was such a powerful cleaner on its own. The idea to use a common ingredient and repackage it as a cleanser made them millions of dollars.

Honda developed an overhead camshaft inline four cylinder engine, from a cylinder that they invented, which had no real purpose at the time. By including it in the engine design for the

CB750 in 1969, it became the industry standard for sports bikes, because of its incredible potential for speed and durability. We have Honda to thank for all the super bikes in the world!

Some innovations that combine knowledge and imagination are strange, but they sell like hotcakes! Just look at the Japanese inventor Bandai, who created the world's first Tamagotchi. These egg-shaped digital toys, had simple LCD screens in black and white, and were very popular in the nineties. The goal of the toy was to look after a pet, by feeding it, playing with it and loving it. After selling over 70 million of these toys, they became the precursor to many online games.

Innovation in Your Life

"The creation of something new is not accomplished by the intellect, but by the play instinct arising from inner necessity. The creative mind plays with the object it loves."
- Carl Jung

What does it mean to be innovative, and do you have that potential inside you? I believe you do, even if you're not sure you have it yet. Innovation is a gift we've all been given, some people just choose to exercise that gift more often than others. And here's the thing. Amidst your life of work, family and general busy-ness – there is never a good time to be innovative. If you wait for a special time, you'll be waiting forever. It's like having kids. Is there really ever a perfect time for that? No!

It's a decision. Innovation is the marriage of creative imagination, an inquisitive mind and the ability to see opportunities, even when they come from unexpected places. Once you land on an idea, you need to run with it – right up until the end. Remember

– you don't need money before an idea, that will come afterwards. Inviting innovation into your life, is like welcoming an old friend back into your life.

When you were a child, you were innovative. You could take a few building blocks and build a pirate ship. You could have hours of fun with an empty cardboard box. Somewhere along the way, we lose this innate belief in our innovative abilities.

Anything can be anything – if you make it that way. I've known some amazing people in my life that have taken little more than a spark of an idea, and turned it into a multi-million dollar business.

Look around you. Everything you see was once an idea, in the mind of a person. Everything from the couch you're sitting on, to the wallet you're using, was initially an innovative idea. When something is new and serves a unique purpose – it's innovative. You want to adopt that spirit of innovation into your own life. Don't confuse innovation with invention, it's much more than that.

Innovation can be a process, a combination of inventions or the improvement of something that already exists. But innovation without persistence, desire and faith is empty and meaningless. It takes hard work, so be prepared to push yourself to do things that are outside your comfort zone. If you risk nothing, you gain nothing.

Innovation is a mindset – and when inspiration strikes like lightning in an open field, you must be ready for it. If you're not, it will be gone. Later on in this chapter, you will learn how to maintain an innovative mindset.

Six People To Emulate

If you're looking for some inspiration, take note of these six innovators and how they used collective knowledge and action to make their ideas come to life.

1. Sir Tim Berners-Lee: The World Wide Web

Ever wondered who created the World Wide Web? Tim Berners-Lee did it in 1989. His innovation would change the world, and be the foundation of tech knowledge that millions of people have built upon over the last 30 years. Tim was fortunate enough to have parents that worked on one of the first commercially built computers in the early days, well before the tech boom.

After receiving a degree in physics, he began working in the technology field – proving once again that formal education isn't always applicable to innovation. In 1989, he worked as a fellow for CERN, the largest internet node in Europe. He says of his innovation, *"I just had to take the hypertext idea and connect it to the Transmission Control Protocol and domain name system ideas and—ta-da!—the World Wide Web."*

Tim was knighted by the Queen for his contributions to the field of technology.

2. Ralph Baer: The Video Game

Ralph Baer invented the first ever video game. While he was working as an engineer creating televisions, he had the idea to incorporate a gaming element to the experience. The idea rooted in his mind, and he told his bosses about it. They weren't interested at all. The idea grew and developed in Ralph's mind for another 15 years. Then he decided to write some notes down about the idea.

After the notes came a schematic, and after that – one month later – came the prototype. Two spots on a screen that bounce from one side to the other. And the rest is history. Today gaming is a billion dollar industry, with almost 90% of all school kids owning and playing on gaming consoles.

Ralph's first gaming console is now on display at the Smithsonian, as a proud part of our technological history.

3. John Logie Baird: The Television

John Baird created the first mechanical television, the earliest version of our now electronic televisions. In the 20's, over a period of three years, John invented a mechanical-electric television, an infrared television system and a way to record it called phonovision. His televisions were the first to broadcast scheduled programs and live broadcasts in the world.

John Baird was a pure visionary, but had an extremely difficult life with many 'failures' and obstacles. He worked on his idea for the television in his attic! Many corporations thought that it was a waste of time and a novelty. His company eventually went bankrupt as other inventors took his idea and improved it electronically. In his final years, Baird still successfully created a high-resolution electronic television that outshone any other in existence.

He has now gone down in history as the father of television, who created one of the most influential mediums of our time.

4. Steve Jobs: Tech Inventor

Steve Jobs invented many of the most successful modern technologies today. He started the Apple Computer company in the 70's, and began producing advanced machines that sold like hotcakes. He invented different font styles for computers, the iPhone, iPad and iPod, and the graphical user interface that all PC's use today.

He also founded Pixar, the world's most successful 3D animation house and the iTunes music store, where fans could buy music for their iPods. The definitive pioneer of mobile technology took innovation to the next level. Steve was adopted as a child and dropped out of college after only one semester. He went on to become an icon in modern tech.

5. Alexander Graham Bell: The Telephone

Alexander Graham Bell invented the first telephone. In his early years, both of his brothers died from tuberculosis. If anything, this only made his will stronger – and he started inventing things when he was a boy of 12, including a dehusking machine that was used in a local mill. After many experiments with the telegraph, Bell became obsessed with the idea of a device that could transmit sound.

He eventually patented an acoustic telegraph and continued developing it until the first ever telephone was created. Proof came when he was able to send sound over long distances, through an underground wire. The Bell Company was born. Without the telephone, we would not have the modern society that we have today.

Bell went down in history as the inventor of the modern telephone, but he also contributed ideas to inventions like the air conditioner, and using solar panels to heat homes.

6. Thomas Edison: The Light Bulb

Thomas Edison was a prolific inventor and innovator that created the light bulb, and contributed to a number of other inventions in his time. Known best for his invention of the light bulb, Edison was doomed to fail 1000 times before finally getting it right.

He owned more than 1000 patents though, including a vote recorder, electrical power, a battery for an electrical car, motion pictures, recorded music and inventions involving the light bulb.

Even after many fierce battles in his life, including competition that nearly crushed his business – Edison continued to contribute to the world of science and discovery. He is regarded by many as the most talented innovator that ever lived. He famously stated,

"I failed my way to success." He was living proof that even though things don't always go as planned, innovation is more important that monetary reward.

Each of these six innovators were inventors, but they were also creative thinkers. Some of their most profound accomplishments came from seeing opportunities in outdated technology, and working towards improved versions of existing products.

If you're going to become an innovator, you should keep these famous innovators in mind. Like you, they came from humble beginnings, and still managed to work their way to the top of their fields.

Keeping Your Eye on Innovation

It should go without saying that in order to stay inspired, you should keep your eye on innovations that are happening all around you. You're lucky enough to live in the technology age, where invention and innovation happen on a daily basis. Whatever your niche field, you need to get into the habit of keeping up to date on what's happening there. Doing this will allow you to see opportunity, where others don't.

A very large niche right now that is expanding rapidly, is the field of social media. Selling on the internet has evolved to become something very beneficial for all businesses, and you need to keep your finger on the pulse of this. Businesses that decided to adopt social marketing early, are now seeing major financial rewards from their quick decision making abilities.

The good news is that social media changes so fast, that you can still get in now and benefit from it. The social media companies and managers that exist in the world will tell you that social media is very important. You need to listen to these people very carefully. Social marketers are innovators. They have to be. It's inherently an applied science, to do with mass marketing, consumer behavior and internet technology.

It's no wonder that social technology is the largest and fastest growing niche in the world. If you look around at the globe's most famous and most influential people, they have all had their hand in social media. Mark Zuckerberg the inventor of Facebook, Steve Jobs the creator of the iPad, Sergey Brin and Larry Page founded Google – all of them are enormously successful because of their interest in social media.

But it's not only the tech geeks that are benefiting from this. Large brands that have cottoned onto the social media gold rush are throwing huge amounts of money at social media. Some of them haven't – and have made millions anyway. Look at Nutella, the famous hazelnut chocolate spread. A fan started their Facebook page, and before long millions of people had joined, which improved their sales so much they hardly invested any money in marketing that year.

Social marketing has huge potential for your business. Regardless of your business, brand or product – it could be the field that opens up new innovations for you. I've seen accountants create 'software as a service' packages, to sell to other accountants – which simplifies project management and data tracking, and automates the process. They've made millions as a result. This can happen for your business.

But first, you have to become active in this niche. Learn all you can about it. There are thousands of ways social marketing can be applied in your niche. You could be the next inventor of a piece of software that revolutionizes your field! Remember, you don't have to have all the technical ability, you just need to have the idea. Think of Henry Ford. He had the ideas and knew which people to approach to make these ideas a reality. The man didn't practically invent anything, but he was the launch pad.

In America alone, experts are saying that businesses that embrace social innovation will be much more successful that those in the future that ignore it. Have you been ignoring everything that's happening online? The internet and social marketing is not the future, it's our present! Hurry up and make it count for your business.

This is how you stay focused and open to new ideas in your niche. All the information in the world is out there, waiting for you to consume and apply it. Make something new, by using your intellect, creative ability and expertise in your niche!

How Do I Become More Innovative?

There are several things you need to pay attention to, if you want to develop an innovative spirit. Take note of these important features.

1. Risk Taking

Nothing ventured is nothing gained. Remember that nugget of ancient wisdom? If you're not constantly pushing to make things happen, because you're afraid of failure – you'll never succeed. Retain your inner voice, and listen to it. You don't need validation from others. All you need is a burning desire and a great idea. The rest is up to you. Take those risks. Make hundreds of mistakes! You only have one life to do your absolute best to be successful.

2. Take Time For Yourself

I've said it before, and I'll say it again. You HAVE to take time for yourself, and the people that matter in your life. If you burn out, you'll never achieve your goals. Be healthy, rest often and approach work with vigor and enthusiasm. This means dedicating your weekends to rest. Absolutely crush it at work from Monday to Friday, then forget about work over the weekend. It's hard to leave business alone, but you must learn to do it, if you want to be an innovator!

3.   Free Your Mind

You have no limitations. Your habits have been made, and they can be broken. While you are working on a day-to-day basis, laboring under enormous pressure – from family, debt, stress, health concerns and more, you must look past these distractions. Life loves to bog us down, and make us forget that we are powerful individuals. When this happens, we adopt a collective, passive mindset – and all original thought and innovation vanishes from our lives.

4.   Persistence and Dedication

You are only a failure if you stop trying. Every great innovator failed miserably thousands of times. Who cares? There is nothing wrong with messing up a few times before you get it right. You must be persistent in your ambition, and tackle all problems like a hungry tiger. Things can only stand in your way if you let them. Don't let them! Dedicate yourself to your one singular goal, and push for it until finally, you achieve that enormous success. It's waiting for you.

5.   Writing Down Your Plan of Action

Take notes, whenever and wherever you can. When you write things down it facilitates creative thought, and helps your mind organize and repurpose important features of your plan. Writing down your plan of action is the first step to bringing an intangible idea into the material world. From there, it's just a matter of planning, time management and dedication.

Nurture these traits in yourself and become a lean mean innovating machine! There is really nothing holding you back but yourself. The world can be yours. Wise up and pursue your destiny in life!

The Amplification of Innovation

Now that you've learned what innovation is all about, let's review the main features.

- Innovation is rare. It's not about general knowledge but specialized knowledge.

- Only with organized knowledge can a superior service be rendered, and wealth itself be harnessed.

- You don't need to possess the knowledge directly, but obtain the knowledge by using people who have expertise in a given area.

- Imagination is the key skill needed, to pair up a good idea with specialized knowledge - then there is no limit to what can happen.

- Innovation is a decision. There is no perfect time to become innovative, it is an ongoing process.

- An innovation can be a process, a combination of inventions or the improvement of something that already exists. But innovation without persistence, desire and faith is empty and meaningless. It takes hard work, so be prepared to push yourself to do things that are outside your comfort zone. If you risk nothing, you gain nothing.

- Keep an eye on innovations in your niche, in particular – on social media marketing and social technology.

- Social marketers are innovators. They have to be. It's inherently an applied science, to do with mass marketing, consumer behavior and internet technology.

- There are thousands of ways social marketing can be applied in your niche. You could be the next inventor of a piece of software that revolutionizes your field! Remember, you don't have to have all the technical ability, you just need to have the idea.

- Take those risks. Make hundreds of mistakes! You only have one life to do your absolute best to be successful.

- Absolutely crush it at work from Monday to Friday, then forget about work over the weekend.

- Free your mind. Life loves to bog us down, and make us forget that we are powerful individuals. When this happens we adopt a collective, passive mindset – and all original thought and innovation vanishes from our lives.

- Dedicate yourself to your one singular goal, and push for it until finally, you achieve that enormous success. It's waiting for you.

- Writing down your plan of action is the first step to bringing an intangible idea into the material world.

CHAPTER NINE

THE WISDOM OF THE FUTURE MINDSET

> *"Again, you can't connect the dots looking forward; you can only connect them looking backwards. So you have to trust that the dots will somehow connect in your future. You have to trust in something - your gut, destiny, life, karma, whatever. This approach has never let me down, and it has made all the difference in my life."*
>
> *– Steve Jobs*

Fake it Until You Make it

The future is coming. It's always coming. By the time it gets here, it's the present. So in fact, the future is simply a concept. But it's something you need to constantly be thinking about, if you want your life to change course. I like to think of the future as a running timeline, with milestones and plans that eventually materialize. It's really the only way you can keep track of where you're going.

If left to its own devices, the future will rush by, and you'll be left in the same position now as you were 10 years ago. Time is not your friend. It escapes even the most careful businessmen. But having a future mindset supports your imagination, and your goals for innovation. Looking ahead, is not so much peering into the future, as planning for it to happen.

That's why a future mindset is really a timeline to action. Or a collection of small actions leading up to an eventual goal. When you can't see ahead, past your current circumstances – you'll never be able to plan for better things. And it all stems from courage. The courage to act, instead of keeping your thoughts contained in your mind. When you have the confidence to be great, you are great. And that brings us to one of my favorite quotes, "Fake it, until you make it!" All it means is that you already know your future, and you're living it now. Expectations, perspective and your belief system are powerful tools to build self-confidence. This self-confidence will carry you, until you can prove that you are who you say you are.

This mantra is really crucial for your future mindset. It's worked for thousands of the world's most successful people. When you behave a certain way, it affects your surroundings and the way people treat you. When you believe that you are something, or that you can achieve something – with all of your mind and soul – your actions change course and start supporting these goals. Have you ever wondered how people are able to do incredible things? Stand in front of a crowd of thousands and give a passionate speech, or create something revolutionary from nowhere? It is self-belief.

Self-belief allows you to do amazing things. It removes the risk of failure, because in your heart you are already a success. You already know that you will succeed – and you project that out into the world. These positive vibes are instrumental in goal achievement. Without them, you couldn't hope to achieve much of anything.

The 'fake it until you make it' principle, empowers you to take on the world. You just don't need validation or support from others, when you have that overwhelming self-belief that a future mindset adopts. Bell had it, so did Jobs and Zuckerberg. The only difference is time. And time as we already know, is relative.

Adopting The Future Mindset

So what is preventing you from adopting the future mindset? Imagine time as two points, and your level of self-confidence as the vehicle you're going to use to get to that second point. One of them is always with you, a starting point to whatever it is you want to do. Where most people fall short, is that they never define the second point. They just don't have the self-belief to understand that they can get there.

Debt makes you agonize about the past, and the present. How will you pay those bills? Why did you have to buy that new dining set last month? When you set out from point A, you're shackled in chains on foot. Every few feet, you have to stop and make a payment. You will never reach your second point! Life is filled with these distractions. Even if you're in a comfortable sedan, because you don't know where the second point is, you always have to stop for directions.

When your self-belief is fully charged, you're in a top-of-the-line Ferrari. You know exactly where point B is, and race to get there. When you have a future mindset, you map out your time correctly, and it is used efficiently. This is highly effective when you finally get that spark of innovation, and an idea is born in your mind. Finally, you can complete your timeline.

Because you know where you're going – you not only get there faster, but you know that you're going to get there. You don't need a GPS system, or a passenger with a map in your front seat. Self-belief fuels your purpose, and you start living your life according to your eventual goals. I don't mean go out into the world and pretend you're rich. Remember, wealth is a by-product of your victories.

It is never the end goal. Your new future mindset might come with a host of challenges. But you'll be able to overcome them, one by one, because you know where point B is! When you get there, it's not a matter of arriving and winning. You simply have to set another point B for yourself. Just as time never ends, your goals should never stop adjusting to your circumstances.

Edison may have invented the light bulb, but he also gave the world thousands of other innovations that future generations built upon. Imagine if he stopped after the light bulb? The world would be very, very different. You should always retain that future mindset – and push yourself to achieve new things, as often as you can. If it's in the future, and you plan for it, it will become your present and your reality!

Accountability and Change

You may have noticed that securing a future mindset is unlike anything you've previously experienced. It can be a big change, and invite a lot of turbulence into your life if you're not careful. While I'm encouraging you to take risks, seize on ideas and go the distance, the truth is that you will suffer many failures as a result. But these failures must not divert you from your main goal.

Accepting change and being accountable for your actions is equally as important as goal setting. Nothing in life is guaranteed. If there is one thing, I'm certain of – it's that you'll have to fight to get where you want to be. It's not going to happen overnight, and it's not going to be easy. Ancient wisdom gives you the tools, but ultimately it's up to you, how to use them.

Always stay mindful of where you are, and how your decisions are affecting your life, and the people around you. Be aware of what you are doing at all times. Be prepared to make adjustments as you go along. Becoming too set in your ways won't give you the results that you need. You'll just end up frustrated and disillusioned.

With accountability comes the realization that there are some things you just can't control. Unfair things happen, and it's not your place to take the blame for them. When these obstacles present themselves, you must give them over to God. He knows what's best for you, and has the power to give you strength when you're feeling defeated.

We've spoken of taking huge leaps of faith and pursuing your goals with all of your might. But you must realize that all goals are made up of baby steps, small victories that eventually make up the whole. By keeping this in mind, you will prevent yourself from lunging forward prematurely, and getting yourself into trouble. Bite off more than you can chew, yes – but spend a good amount of time chewing to make up for that.

Finally, accept that sometimes people will be against you. You might be turned down repeatedly, laughed at or ridiculed – and it will test your resolve. This is the time you must find your inner voice and stick to your guns. There is no success without perseverance, and no achievement without failure.

I'm trying to empower you with these ancient secrets, and caution you at the same time. We all fall victim to excitement, and rash decisions, but you must be vigilant about your process. That's why I've been calling it a plan. When you have everything written down, you'll be able to see where you went wrong and change it. Don't hasten into things and forget to take stock of where you are.

Embracing Change and Responsibility

On your journey to achievement, you will question your competence, your mission, your motivations and your intentions. This is a natural process. It takes a responsible, mindful person to admit when they have failed, or alter something that hasn't worked.

If you continue to do the same things over and over, you will always get the same end result. In business, this can be catastrophic.

Maintaining a future mindset is great, but it mustn't come at the expense of your present. Be responsible for your actions, and be proactive about changing them as needed.

How can you become more accountable in your life? It's simple. Question everything you do, and never stop. Listen to what others tell you, but decide for yourself whether it is relevant or not. When you make a decision, stand by that decision and accept whatever happens because of it.

Success is not a race. While there is a start, there is no finish line. It will be the collective power of your achievements that constitutes the success you have in life. Each achievement is a goal realized. Change can be positive or negative, according to your decisions. So weigh these decisions carefully. Never act out of greed or selfishness and pray over each decision.

The way you live right now is a product of your decisions. You are responsible for them. The same can be said about your future achievements. You will find that the deeper you get into goal attainment, the more fulfilling life becomes. The key here, is to not make it the center of your life.

Money and Accountability

I believe that along this torrid path, you must maintain a giving heart to reach your goals. When you're given money, it's

148

your responsibility to channel that money into worthwhile causes. Accountability with money is a big one. The person with a future mindset always remembers the plights of people in the present.

While you are on a journey of self-discovery and achievement, it's up to you to inspire others to do the same. Help people financially when you can, and set them upon their own journey. Gods wants us to be accountable, not only for ourselves and our families, but for the people around us.

It is one of the reasons why I've written this book. It's my heart's desire to give back, and inspire you to do great things. I am investing in your future, so that you can invest in the future of others. If we all just took the time to do this, imagine what we could achieve together! As you elevate yourself, so should you elevate others in your wake. Remember that, and keep it close.

Perseverance and Goal Attainment

Without oxen a stable stays clean, but you need a strong ox for a large harvest.
Proverbs 14:4:

What areas of your life have you been leaving 'clean?' What portions of your life, have you let atrophy for fear of failure? What opportunities have you let pass you by because of the capital that would have been required? What investments could you make in your life, in your families future, in others that you passed over for the sake of muddying the stables?

There are a lot of things in life that I have personally excelled at, and others that, like anyone, have struggled with, but pushing life to the limit and going HUGE has never been one of my struggles. I grew up learning early on, that people, who did barely enough to get by, were rewarded with 'nothing – no reward at all.'

I also learned that people who just did a good job, didn't get a good reward, but just an okay return for their efforts! That's why people that work hard are not always successful. The act of working hard is not enough to secure success. Instead you have to work hard at the right things, with the right mindset – and according to a solid timeline! You have got to have that IDEA to work towards.

You can also mess it up by working too hard. If you don't rest enough, you'll burn out – and all creativity and innovation will leave you. Then you'll be stuck laboring away at a job, doing the same things everyday – and doing them well – but not well enough for any significant change or positive reward.

Get this, people who expanded on their service in mass, those who give absolute excellence, get a 'good reward.' If you want it all, I mean if you want to absolutely come away with a life, married in happiness and success, you have to live a little! You need an ox and you need to feed it well.

My background is real estate. I have made a fantastic living as an owner of real estate and as a messenger to help others buy it. I have seen so many people, who had so many opportunities to do great things - go absolutely nowhere, because fear of risk, or fear of the unknown. The intent focus on simply playing it safe kept them from executing their destiny. Take inventory on your life today.

What areas have you played too safe? What areas have you held your cards too close and let opportunity pass you by? If you are reading this, then it's not too late to get an ox into the stable and get after an amazing harvest.

In the real estate boom in 2004, Las Vegas' home values went completely off the charts. It wasn't uncommon for a home to be $200k one week and then two short weeks later, a builder to raise the price $15 or $20,000 more!

If you showed up at a new home tract, the parking lots looked like a busy day at a shopping mall, and these were fraught with lotteries - just to have a chance to buy a home! It was so bad, that it was nearly impossible for anyone to buy a home. Homes were turning quickly. I saw buyer's buy homes, and then decide they needed to move to another market, and sell the home almost immediately to make $10,000 overnight.

I was of the mindset that everyone else had at the time. Real estate had never seen decline, and in my mind along with the rest of America, it would always go up. A good friend of mine used to always call me a 'Cowboy' in business. I always jump into something and when I am personally invested, I go to the moon with it, and I have had to learn the hard way to temper that attitude back.

Being in the business, I knew Las Vegas was heavily inflated due to heavy interest from the west coast markets; buyers from the west found us a bargain and bought Vegas up like it was a drug. I also knew in mid 2004 that Vegas would soon become appealing, and that these buyers would go somewhere else to meet their real estate objectives. But WHERE would they go?

I looked at the closest local markets that looked to be sound and ideal for growth. Phoenix fitted the bill. I was amazed at the growth of that valley, and the amount of businesses that were headquartered there, or were slated to move there soon. I was most interested in the NW and West valleys. I interviewed an agent there, and took my family and a couple of members of my team, and off we went.

Creating New Goals From Opportunity

That summer in Phoenix was a complete reversal to what I was used to. If you pulled up to a new home track, there wasn't a soul there!

You were welcomed and served, where in Vegas, you were put in a line! I went in, looked around, told the sales agent about the home I wanted, cut them a check, and left – all in about 20 minutes. I did this 5 times over in one day, risked about $13k in deposits to have these homes built, and went back to Vegas.

Months later, we went back to Phoenix to start picking out options for these homes, and those parking lots were just as I suspected that they would be – completely slammed.

The west coast markets had moved straight over Vegas almost in succession, and had started to hit Phoenix! Homes that I purchased, had the same process of elevating prices taking place! How exciting. In a years' time, each one of those homes went up from $50 to over $100,000 each!

Allow me for a second to temper this statement. It would be ridiculous to run head long into a venture or idea without proper *preparation.* Later on in the same chapter – *Proverbs 14:16, says – The wise are cautious and avoid danger; fools plunge ahead with reckless confidence.* There is a big difference between jumping at every idea or opportunity that comes your way, and applying your intellect and research ability before you forge ahead.

You have to be able to measure the risks involved and manage them accordingly. If they seem viable, and hold a lot of potential – then act on them. But don't invest your time and money on ideas that have no real merit. As with anything, you must first weigh the pros and cons, and determine if your risk is viable. That's just good business.

There is a big difference between igniting desire in your life to the absolute max – allowing your mind to vault headlong into a thing without any fear of failure, without any predisposition to failure. This is the essence of gaining what you want. However, a focused, mind-controlled person, does not run the engine of desire into the wall of foolishness.

Iron sharpens iron and those who attain greatness make sure that wisdom is channeled into a project. Before I went to Arizona, I spent several weekends researching area markets. The money wasn't made by the fact that I jumped into my car and ran into the sales office flashing my money around so that I could acquire a property.

Being a cowboy ONLY pays off if you measure and inspect the thing, constantly. Winning is a LOT of fun, but make sure that you don't set up a series of colossal wins into an ending failure. Don't do damage to your business or your name - because you focused so heavily on cash drivers, success, and various passions, in a careless fashion.

I like to think of myself as a big picture person or a 'cash cow' business guy. I like to throw the craziest things on the wall, sell myself completely into the business, and cut the lifeboats loose!

The unfortunate part of this, is that the small moving parts can be overlooked and can do damage to the plan. This can reverse your success in a given area. Everything must be monitored. You may have heard the statement, 'you have to measure what you manage.'

Most people have a tendency to be either task oriented or detail oriented. Either is fine, but one specific value will serve you more in a specific position. If you are hiring a bookkeeper and you put a task-oriented person in that position, then you will get someone who can reconcile your accounts in record time, but they will mess up the numbers quickly!

If you get a detail oriented person, to do a simple data entry job, they will take a painstaking amount of time but tell you "yeah, it will be done right though!" It's important to know where you fall, and play to these strengths. It's only when you can do this that persistence will pay off, and you'll reach your defined goals.

The Amplification of the Future Mindset

Review the things that will help you create and maintain a future mindset. When you need to, return to this page for inspiration.

- Having a future mindset supports your imagination, and your goals for innovation. Looking ahead, is not so much peering into the future, as planning for it to happen.

- When you have the confidence to be great, you are great.

- "Fake it, until you make it!" You already know your future, and you're living it now. Expectations, perspective and your belief system are powerful tools to build self-confidence. This self-confidence will carry you, until you can prove that you are, who you say you are.

- Self-belief allows you to do amazing things. It removes the risk of failure, because in your heart you're already a success. You already know that you'll succeed – and you project that out into the world.

- Define your end goal, so that you can build up the self-confidence to get there.

- Self-belief fuels your purpose, and you start living your life according to your eventual goals.

- Accepting change and being accountable for your actions is equally as important as goal setting. Nothing in life is guaranteed. If there's one thing I'm certain of – it's that you'll have to fight to get where you want to be.

- Maintaining a future mindset is great, but it mustn't come at the expense of your present. Be responsible for your actions, and be proactive about changing them as needed.

- The act of working hard is not enough to secure success. Instead, you have to work hard at the right things, with the right mindset – and according to a solid timeline! You have got to have that IDEA to work towards.

- You are accountable for the money you earn, give back as much as you can to those who need it. As you elevate yourself, so should you elevate those around you.

- *Proverbs 14:16, says - The wise are cautious and avoid danger; fools plunge ahead with reckless confidence.*

- Being a cowboy ONLY pays off if you measure and inspect the thing, constantly. Winning is a LOT of fun, but make sure that you don't set up a series of colossal wins into an ending failure.

- Everything must be monitored. 'You have to measure what you manage.'

CHAPTER TEN

THE WISDOM OF HAPPINESS FIRST

Happiness is not a matter of good fortune or worldly possessions. It's a mental attitude. It comes from appreciating what we have, instead of being miserable about what we don't have. It's so simple? Yet so hard for the human mind to comprehend.

– Anon

Understanding Happiness

People seek happiness their entire lives, and never find it. We are told that without money and material wealth – we can never be happy. As a result, most of us obsess about the things we don't have, instead of concentrating on the things we do have. Interestingly enough, scientific research claims that lower income families are far happier than higher income groups.

This begs the question – if money can't buy you happiness, what can? You've probably heard that happiness is a state of mind. That's true. But it's a reactive state of mind. You can make the choice to be happy in life, but if you're not living to your full potential, with some important core factors in mind – this mindset will change with your circumstances.

Personally, I believe that happiness is the result of using your God given talents, and nurturing a giving heart. There has to be a balance with everything in life – so it makes sense that the more you acquire, the more you should help others. Happiness is not a selfish pursuit. It's the collection of psychological and social factors that form your mindset.

A friend once told me that he tries to live life in the moment as best he can. He heard that happiness isn't a continuous feeling, it's a combination of the right circumstances and an overwhelming realization. When you achieve something, that moment directly afterwards – you're happy. When you help someone, the same thing happens. I found this perspective quite interesting.

We all have different ideas on what makes a person happy. Or more to the point, what makes you happy. That's why I feel that being proactive or useful is psychologically uplifting, as is connecting with people on a social level. Now here is something fascinating – the definition of happiness from a psychology research paper: "Happiness is the degree to which a person evaluates the overall quality of his present life-as-a-whole positively. In other words, how much the person likes the life he/she leads." I loved this definition because it proves two things. The first, is that you can't be happy if you're not doing what you love. You need to enjoy the work you do to be satisfied with your life.

Secondly, you can't be happy if you're not working selflessly. Giving back to people that need help, builds your self-confidence and feeds your soul. It reminds you that with enough effort, you have the power to change lives.

Happiness is the reality that you create for yourself. In an ideal world, this means financial reward, and the power to effect positive change in people's lives.

The Definition of Happiness

We all have different paths we need to take in life. What you haven't realized yet, is that all of our paths pursue the same thing – happiness. When you dream about having more money, or being able to achieve more, you're actually dreaming about being happier. The funny thing is that money doesn't always amount to happiness. It often brings even more problems into your life.

There is a persistent idea of happiness as something that can be attained in the future. The problem with thinking this way is that the future never comes. True happiness is not a destination, it's a pursuit. One that lasts a lifetime. So, this begs the question – what are you doing right now to be happy? Don't hold happiness to some lofty ideal of the perfect life. Seek it now, in your everyday dealings.

Create moments of happiness that drive you forward, and soon you'll find that your life is happier for it. This comes from improving yourself, and improving the lives of others. Remember that we all live in the reality that we ourselves have created. Perhaps, what you've been looking for all this time has been in your reach, but you've been too distracted to notice.

I think the true definition of happiness is a mixture of self-actualization and determination – to be positive, hard working and endlessly charitable. When we can overcome the idea that happiness is not some future destination, and that helping people is not something only wealthy people can do – our lives change.

Happiness is what we are all after, yet we repeatedly put it on the backburner! When you don't allow time for happiness in your life, you'll never achieve it. You need to learn the ancient wisdom of putting happiness first in your life. Appreciate all that's good in your life, and try to improve it. Take steps to change the things in your life you don't like. And at every step, give yourself time to be happy.

The Fear of Failure

"One who fears failure limits his activities. Failure is only the opportunity to more intelligently begin again."
– Henry Ford

The fear of failure is something we all experience in our lives. It manifests in many ways, but always has the same result – not taking action. Dismissal, denial, anxiety, helplessness and panic are all products of fear. You might think that you take risks –but do you? Is there a voice in your head that tells you its okay not to do something because it will be too hard to achieve?

The fear of failure is flat out the biggest threat to your happiness. No great man or woman has ever given into fear, because something seemed too tough. It's the root cause of procrastination and laziness.

When you don't act upon your ideas, they have no chance of ever becoming a reality. Society teaches us to fear failure, like it will ruin your life, and prevent you from being happy.

This is one of the largest most distasteful lies we are taught to believe. From a young age in school – we're shown that achievement is everything, and failure is nothing. Or more to the point, if we try hard and fail, we get the same result that we would've experienced, if we hadn't tried at all. So we enter life believing it's better to not try, and save yourself the trouble!

You've heard the old saying "There's nothing to fear, but fear itself." And this nugget of ancient wisdom should be taken to heart. Fear prevents courage and action, and will stunt your ideas. It will prevent you from ever reaching your true potential. Time and time again, it will undermine your pursuit of happiness. Ignoring fear and charging forward is certainly the greatest lesson you will ever learn.

Now here's a question for you:

What would you attempt to do, if you knew you couldn't fail?

You would have lived a very different life. I learned early that failure doesn't exist. Some paths are long, and some are short, but they all lead to success. If you can put 'failure' into perspective, you'll never have to worry about it again. I see each failure as another stone along the path.

You might only need one stone, to get it right. You might need 50. The commonality here is that you will need these stones. Without them, there is no path. If you don't have a path, how can you find your way to success?

Failure is such an ugly word. Instead, think of it as 'attempts at success.' As I've mentioned before, failure is only complete when you stop trying.

Most people stop trying because they are scared of failure. Which is ironic, because stopping is what causes them to fail! If they had just kept on learning, changing and evolving – success could have been around the corner.

How To Overcome Your Fear of Failure

If you've recognized a fear of failure in yourself – you're not alone. It still sneaks up on me sometimes, and I have to pray about it to keep going. But your mindset has got to change, in a powerful, permanent manner. You need to become fearless, so that you are able to embrace happiness completely.

Put In The Hours

When an idea first strikes your mind, it's held together only with the vaguest notions, and is limited by your current knowledge. If you can't possibly see a way to make it a reality, put in the hours. Do your research. You'll be surprised at how much sense something can make, when you take the time to check it out.

Reality Check

Think carefully about the consequences of your actions. If you pursue this dream, what will it cost you? I'm not talking about the 'false' perceptions that we all scare ourselves with, I'm talking about reality. If you really go full force, and it doesn't work out – what's the worst that can happen? So you lose some money. Your life won't be over!

As long as you live and breathe, opportunities are out there. It's a lot less scary when you realize you're not risking everything. Time for a reality check.

Success Check

If you work hard, plan well and achieve your goals – how will it change your life? Before you're bogged down with fear, consider the implications of not running with your new idea. There's no such thing as putting all of your eggs into one basket. For every idea, there is an incredible outcome. If you pursue that with all of your might, you will achieve it. Can you afford to give that up?

Create a Plan B

If you're really worried about the outcome of your goals, create a plan B. Success is 10% talent, and 90% planning. If you want to sidestep a failure, then don't plan to fail – even if something does go awry. In business, this is called a contingency plan. Manage your risk, and reduce the chance of a disappointing outcome. When I make an investment, I plan to win across the board. It's just *how much* I'll win, that then comes into question!

Get over your fear of failure. It's ruining your chances at happiness, and keeping you from your full potential!

A Balanced Life of Joy

There's something to be said about living a happy life. I've focused a lot on goal attainment and financial success in this book, but if your priorities are different – then go with your heart. Happiness is the eventual goal, for all of us. To achieve this, you must live a balanced life of joy. Here's an inspiring parable, written by the noted author Paulo Coelho, on happiness.

The Happiness Parable: Paulo Coelho

An American investment banker was at the pier of a small coastal Mexican village, when a small boat with just one fisherman docked. Inside the small boat were several large yellow fin tuna. The American complimented the Mexican on the quality of his fish and asked how long it took to catch them.

The Mexican replied, "Only a little while."

The American then asked why he didn't stay out longer and catch more fish?

The Mexican said he had enough to support his family's immediate needs.

The American then asked, "But what do you do with the rest of your time?"

The Mexican fisherman said, "I sleep late, fish a little, play with my children, take siestas with my wife, Maria, stroll into the village each evening where I sip wine, and play guitar with my amigos. I have a full and busy life."

The American scoffed, "I am a Harvard MBA and could help you. You should spend more time fishing and with the proceeds, buy a bigger boat. With the proceeds from the bigger boat, you could buy several boats, eventually you would have a fleet of fishing boats. Instead of selling your catch to a middleman you would sell directly to the processor, eventually opening your own cannery. You would control the product, processing, and distribution. You would need to leave this small coastal fishing village and move to Mexico City, then LA and eventually New York City, where you will run your expanding enterprise."

The Mexican fisherman asked, "But, how long will this al take?"

To which the American replied, "15 – 20 years."

"But what then?" Asked the Mexican.

The American laughed and said, "That's the best part. When the time is right you would announce an IPO and sell your company stock to the public and become very rich, you would make millions!"

"Millions – then what?"

The American said, "Then you would retire. Move to a small coastal fishing village where you would sleep late, fish a little, play with your grandkids, take siestas with your wife, stroll to the village in the evenings where you could sip wine and play your guitar with your amigos."

This parable has always inspired me. It shows the contrast between what modern society believes to be success and happiness, and what a simplified version of happiness actually is. The Mexican already understood what life was about. He lived in the moment, on a day-to-day basis – happy and fulfilled. The investment banker saw nothing but small thinking and a small life.

He didn't understand that the Mexican had already attained true happiness, and that none of that other stuff was necessary. It's a great parable to keep in mind, when you're working towards what you desire in life. Whether it's a successful business, great investments, a happy marriage or well rounded children. At the end of the day, you decide where to draw the line.

Balance in Your Life

Always stay true to yourself, and walk in your light. Ignore what others say about your plans, or their claims to have achieved happiness. Everyone has their own unique balance. For you, perhaps it's working less and spending more time with your family. For the next person, it could be achieving those incredible career goals, while still making time for their family.

Your priorities are important. Just remember that happiness comes first, not money. Money is just a means to attain happiness. You should already be living with these excellent moments of joy. Without them, you can never hope to be successful. Balance is the key to happiness. Let me explain.

A single-minded pursuit for anything is both damaging and inefficient. I'm very career driven, but I realized that at the end of the day – without a family, my life would be meaningless. So I spend a great deal of energy making sure that my family is happy, and that I spend every weekend with them.

If I took all this information to heart, that I've written in this book – and spent it on one thing – the pursuit of money, my life would fall apart. I'd lose my wife, my kids and all the money in the world couldn't replace them. Instead, I focus on balance. You need to realize balance is that important.

It's VERY tempting to throw yourself into your ideas and ignore everyone around you. It's easy to forget that others need your help. But selfish goals, aren't goals at all. If you've been burning the candle at both ends and have forgotten that happiness comes first – this is your reality check.

Helping others, being with your family, spending time with friends – these are the things that make you happy. Happiness FIRST.

The Amplification of Happiness

Happiness is everything. When you're feeling lost, review these ways to make happiness first in your life.

- Happiness is a reactive state of mind. It's the result of using your God given talents, and nurturing a giving heart. There has to be a balance with everything in life – so it makes sense that the more you acquire, the more you should help others. Happiness is *not* a selfish pursuit.

- You can't be happy if you're not doing what you love. You need to enjoy the work you do to be satisfied with your life. And you can't be happy if you're not working selflessly.

- There is a persistent idea of happiness as something that can be attained in the future. The problem with thinking this way, is that the future never comes. True happiness is not a destination, it's a pursuit. One that lasts a lifetime.

- When we can overcome the idea that happiness is not some future destination, and that helping people is not something only wealthy people can do – our lives change.

• Happiness should always come FIRST

• The fear of failure is flat out the biggest threat to your happiness. No great man or woman has ever given in to fear, because something seemed too tough. It's the root cause of procrastination and laziness.

• Fear prevents courage and action, and will stunt your ideas. It will prevent you from ever reaching your true potential. Time and time again, it will undermine your pursuit of happiness. Ignoring fear and charging forward is certainly the greatest lesson you will ever learn.

• Each failure is another stone along the path to success. You might only need one stone, to get it right. You might need 50. The commonality here is that you will need these stones. Without them, there is no path. If you don't have a path, how can you find your way to success?

• Remember the parable of the investment banker and the Mexican man. Happiness can be simple, when uncomplicated by the world around you.

• It's VERY tempting to throw yourself into your ideas and ignore everyone around you. It's easy to forget that others need your help. But selfish goals, aren't goals at all.

CHAPTER ELEVEN

THE WISDOM OF PREPARATION

"Before anything else, preparation is the key to success."
–Alexander Graham Bell

The Millionaire Morning

There are thousands of great leaders that have commented on the importance of preparation. Not in the traditional sense, of going to school, or getting a degree – but preparing for an idea to become successful. This sentiment has even given rise to a common saying – *If you have an idea and you prepare for failure, instead of success, you'll achieve the one you prepared for.*

This is the practical section of my book. While all of these ancient secrets can be used in the real world, these are of a more practical nature.

I like to call the first one, the millionaire morning. I've been fortunate enough to learn a lot from people far more successful than I am, and there are patterns of behavior I've noticed in all of them. I believe habits breed success, so I'm going to share them with you.

To fully prepare for your life of success, you MUST focus on your physical, mental and spiritual health.

I've never met anyone that has done anything great with their lives that slept late whenever they got the chance. To be successful, you need to adopt the lifestyle of successful people. People who are motivated don't mess around. They don't waste time. Every second is a gift from God, and you better believe they're going to use it wisely. So pay attention!

Every morning you need to focus on exercise. There is always time before you get ready, where you can add in an hour for personal fitness and health. Waking up early, and taking on an exercise routine is a fantastic way to stay in shape, maintain high energy and get those ideas flowing. There is nothing more beneficial than getting up early, and getting your heart pumping.

Overcome Bad Habits

It's amazing how one small change can affect your life. Like many Americans, you probably roll out of bed, giving you the exact amount of time you need to get ready and rush to work. You grab a hasty, carb-based breakfast and get to work half asleep. You then try to wake yourself up with coffee, and pile through the day until you get to go home. Then you make or order dinner, sit at the TV, and go to bed.

If you don't start your day prepared, how do you ever expect anything to change?

You want your day to start with a bang, so that by the time you get to work, you're in top gear – and can get things done, fast and efficiently. This means never oversleeping again. Sleeping too much drains your energy and slows your mind. I've never met a millionaire that doesn't wake up early to work out and feel great!

It's vital to their day. If they aren't fully awake and rearing to go, hours will be wasted of their time. And millionaires don't waste time. Best of all, this early morning exercise is exactly what your mind needs to feel good, open and alert.

Wake up every single day and spend an hour exercising. You can alternate between cycling, walking or jogging – even bouncing on a trampoline! It's best to do this every day, on weekends too. After a week or so of doing this, your body will adjust – and then the magic happens.

Suddenly, you're not tired when you wake up. Your body needs to get moving. When you skip an early morning workout, you regret it! It's a great way to release stress and invite positive energy into your day. If you are overweight, it will help sort out your negative self-image. If you are underweight, it will make you stronger.

Exercising does amazing things for your day. It's important to do this exercise at the same time daily, with a positive attitude. You'll begin to feel the effects almost immediately. Millionaires carefully prepare their bodies and minds for success each morning because it is vital to their day!

Prepare for your day. Break those lazy habits. Laziness is not the breeding ground of success. Get up, work out and make it happen! Be proactive.

Living Your Personal and Business Culture

As you pursue your own business goals, it will become clear that your personal life and business life are entwined. This is especially true for business owners, who practically live for their businesses. If you haven't spent any time establishing your business culture, then the time is now. It can do a lot for you, and will make living a balanced life easier than if it remains undefined.

This is another great lesson in preparing for success.

You've seen or heard of businesses that promote a certain kind of culture – and these tend to be the businesses that are the most successful. Just take a look at Google, as a great example. Their offices are incredible! They promote play, just as much as they promote work. So – what is business culture?

When you build a company, it is made up of what you believe a company should be. Like a country, it retains its own form of cultural appeal. Perhaps you have a break room, or invite your employees to do lunch as a team every month. These little motivators are what make up your culture.

If you business culture is undefined so far, then here are some things to think about:

- What sort of employees do you want to attract?
- What values do you want to instill in your employees, and promote to your clients?
- How much responsibility do you assign your employees?
- What is your involvement, and do you delegate tasks?
- What kind of behaviors do you want to encourage?

Until now, your company culture has evolved without your input. But creating a company culture depends on preparation. There are so many reasons to do this. The largest, is of course that it will determine the kind of people that are attracted to your company. It will influence how long people work for you, and how loyal they are. It can improve productivity and promote certain behaviors.

Imagine a small company whose success relies on very bright employees that work extremely hard. This sort of company requires a lot of team work to function. It makes sense then, that you should incorporate unique break times, and team building opportunities into your business culture.

Now, imagine that you need to hire one of these bright people. They have options. What is going to make your company stand out? The internal company culture! This person will see and hear about the breaks that they are allowed to game, read, relax or watch television. They'll be interested in the company 'outings' that you promote.

If the current team you have seems happy and focused, and there's a great work environment happening, they'll choose your company over other options. Your business culture is what makes your business unique. It's equally as important as any business plan. Laying this foundation for success is of enormous importance, if you want to build a successful business.

So what does it mean to live your personal and business culture? They are inevitably linked. It means that you need to make an effort with the people that work for you. You need to get to know them socially, in a non-business context. By instilling your personal beliefs into your business, you're setting yourself up for major success.

Always keep in mind how your employees feel about the working conditions in your business!

The Millionaire Physique

We've spoken about exercise and the importance of keeping fit, and exercising each morning. But there's more to success than exercise. In fact, there is a whole lot more! One of the ways you can prepare yourself for success is by looking after your health. This begins with proper nutrition, or what I like to call the millionaire diet!

Food plays an essential role in our metabolism, weight and overall health. It can be used as medicine. Either to keep your body in great condition, or it can destroy your health, thanks to massive weight gain from bad nutritional choices. Most of us have very little time to cook, so we take the easy route – fast food!

The irony here is that fast food is actually the fast track to ill health and disease. Highly motivated people take the time to care about their health. There is no way they'd spend money ruining it.

And that's what you're doing, every time you go for the easy option. But successful people aren't about what's easy. In fact, as soon as they make any money, they hire nutritionists to create the perfect diet for them, so that they can continue doing what they're good at: business. Food directly affects how you feel, and the amount of energy that you have.

Too much fast food and you will never have the energy required to turn an idea into reality! When you're overweight and exhausted, it's so easy to go back to your passive mindset. Go to work. Watch TV. Eat. Never take risks, never do anything outside your comfort zone. Society encourages bad behavior. It's up to you to correct that behavior by choosing to go on a healthy diet.

The diet that works best for me is called the Mediterranean Diet. It's really not complex, and because it's promoted as a 'lifestyle change' instead of a diet, there's never an end to it. This discourages yo-yo dieting and relapsing into bad habits. If you're going to eat something bad – eat it! But then pick up where you left off.

That's what I love about the Mediterranean Diet. There's no guilt and no expectations. It's helped me achieve that Millionaire physique, without having to hire some nutritionist to create a diet plan for me. The premise is simple: give up the food that makes you fat and ill, and embrace the food that charges your body!

Yes friends – that means no more fast food. It's high in fat, and contains all kinds of terrible things, like MSG. Can you imagine working your butt off to become successful, and then you're diagnosed with cancer or diabetes – because of the way you've been eating! Fast food is trouble, and it has no place in your life.

Instead, take some principles from the Mediterranean Diet. It focuses on balancing your hormones, so that you're less hungry, and achieve greater health – sooner than other diets. You can eat a whole host of tasty foods, especially the ones that promote hormone balance.

The basis for this diet is to commit to eating lots of wonderful fruits, veggies and healthy meats. Like I said, it's a common sense diet. It discourages fast food, deserts and sugar-laden items like ice cream and soda. You will be amazed at how good you feel once you stop experiencing sugar crashes and cravings.

Another well-known diet that is effective in reversing the negative issues brought on by obesity is the HCG Diet.

The HCG Diet was created by Dr. Simeons in the 1950's and has gained a lot of popularity over the past few years. In his book -Pounds & Inches, Dr. Simeons discusses his findings of HCG or human chorionic gonadotropin as an effective weight loss system. This book is easily available online.

Please note, that in no way am I affiliated to either the Mediterranean or the HCG Diet. But, I do know from personal experience that these diets are effective in dealing with weight loss.

Getting your millionaire physique, is preparing for your busy, balanced life of success. Trust me when I say the results are remarkable. Once I was fast food free, and not struggling for energy anymore – the opportunities were all over the place! As horrible as it sounds, you can't be focused and successful when you're lazy. It's going to take the same amount of effort losing your weight, as it will to become successful.

It's up to you to decide how difficult or how easy it is. Personally, I find that once I've made a commitment to something, it's actually very easy. The hard part, is never losing focus, and keeping the things that matter in perspective. Your health and wellbeing is at the top of that list. Better yourself now, and it will all be worth it.

What Kind of Things Should I Eat?

The best answer, is the kind of stuff you actually never feel like eating! Nice lean or white meat, complimented with vegetables is great for dinner. Ryvita is much better for you than bread, so have that for lunch. Eat five fruits a day. If you feel like you're going to die of starvation, buy a healthy protein supplement, and have that as a snack during the day.

Try not to eat normal potatoes, instead eat sweet potatoes. Stay away from white starches. These are really all basic bits of diet knowledge that you should already know. You just haven't thought to apply them to your life. The Mediterranean Diet and How To Balance Your Hormones is available for sale, if you want to know more about it.

I recommend getting your hands on that book, if you want some serious, practical diet advice. Better yet, it's advice that works, because it's all grounded in medical knowledge. Get your millionaire physique and prepare for your success. Remember, failing to plan, is planning to fail!

Absorbing World Knowledge

There's a world of knowledge out there, waiting to be used for your benefit. The best way to promote ideas and find opportunities, is to always stay in touch with what's happening in the world. When you learn to do this, you'll find that you really don't have any limits.

The Internet is a great example. Ask it a question, and you get an educated answer from some of the brightest minds in the world.

There are many ways you can improve your business and expand your horizons. Remember, nothing is out of reach – if you think big!

How About a Call Center?

There's a reason why you're still bothered a few times a week from people trying to sell you stuff from call centers. They work. While most people harbor animosity towards call center staff, it really doesn't have to be that way. How can you integrate a call center into your business to improve your bottom line?

How can you bring new innovations to your call center? Everyone has been on the receiving end of a sales call. Can you make this work for your business? These are the kinds of opportunities that you should be thinking about. Nothing is set in stone. You need to evolve, and think laterally about your business potential.

Look Into Buy Sell Agreements

There's value in buy sell agreements you know. If you're in partnership with someone else, give them the option of being bought out. It works both ways. One day if your business becomes too big, and you're fired or injured – this could cover you financially. Just look at what happened to Steve Jobs. He founded Apple, and was then fired from it!

Think about buy sell agreements for a while to see what you come up with.

Research and Implement Social Media Campaigns

We've spoken previously about the value of social media and internet marketing. This is one field you don't want to skip. The opportunities here are virtually limitless. Do as much research as you can into social media, and then try and find a social media company to manage it for you.

The best companies will be able to come up with a unique social strategy for you, and then implement it over a period of time. They'll send you reports and you'll be able to see how they're improving your online presence – and earning you more money via social sites like Facebook, LinkedIn, Google+ and Twitter.

Do yourself a favor and listen to the social media guy!

Get Into Podcasting

Imagine having your own personal audio university at your fingertips. If you've been worried about all this extra time you need, then look into podcasting. I love it! A podcast is a fancy word for a multimedia file that can combine sounds, visuals and text. Mainly, they are audio files that you can listen to on your iPod, computer or mobile device.

There are so many great business podcasters out there, that you'll never stop learning. When you get up for your morning exercise, just pop in your earphones and listen to a few of these inspirational speakers. You can download audio lessons that teach you just about anything under the sun!

I'd also investigate this medium as a marketing tool. Radio is pretty much dead, but podcasting is new, innovative and on the rise. Why not give your business a human voice by investing in some online podcasting? There's a thought!

Try Email Marketing and List Building

There's a huge world out there on the internet. They say if you can keep in constant contact with your clients, then you can earn additional income with repeat business. It's true, and the stats prove it. Marketing via email has come a long way from the old 'spam' emails we used to get in our inboxes.

Build your list of subscribers through your business website, and send them weekly emails. You can track these emails, what people click on, what they download or like – and over time, market to them based on data and analytics. Imagine if instead of wasting money on that hit and miss print ad, you focused that investment on email marketing? The returns would be far more significant.

Getting The Most From The World

To absorb world knowledge means to keep abreast of trends and innovations. When you do this, you are exposed to limitless possibilities. It also helps keep things in context for you. You'll know more about the economy, politics and what's happening in the financial sector.

When you constantly analyze the trends in your own niche, you'll be able to predict dips in the market, or when something big is going to happen. Keep questioning yourself at every step. There's nothing wrong with digging your feet in, and being relentless in your pursuit of that perfect idea.

External sources will certainly help you with that. But you must keep an open mind, especially where new technology is involved. I knew quite a successful businessman who worked in the financial sector. During the recession a few years ago, his business came close to closing. Instead of giving up, he looked into every possible route to bring in more money.

At the time there was a new technology burgeoning – the mobile application. He took a big chance, and invested what little capital he had into creating an application that could be used by Forex traders. His risk paid off. The mobile application sold thousands of copies, and kept his business open during those rougher months.

The moral of the story is that the world holds many solutions for us, if we care to look for them. To ignore that there are other things going on, is not only ignorant, but short sighted. You have to learn to grab the most from the world, as often as you can. It takes extra work and effort, but that effort pays off big time!

Try new things. Stay innovative and curious. Ancient wisdom tells us that we are all part of the same world, and equally affected by its changes. Prepare for your life of success, and you'll get there – fast!

The Amplification of Preparation

Need some inspiration on preparation? Ancient wisdom tells us that we can't achieve anything if we are ill prepared. Let's review.

- To fully prepare for your life of success, you MUST focus on your physical, mental and spiritual health.

- To be successful, you need to adopt the lifestyle of successful people. People who are motivated don't mess around. They don't waste time. Every second is a gift from God, and you better believe they're going to use it wisely.

- Waking up early, and taking on an exercise routine is a fantastic way to stay in shape, maintain high energy and get those ideas flowing.

- Prepare for your day. Break those lazy habits. Laziness is not the breeding ground of success. Get up, work out and make it happen! Be proactive.

- When you build a company, it is made up of what you believe a company should be. Like a country, it retains its own form of cultural appeal. Make yours count.

- Food plays an essential role in our metabolism, weight and overall health. It can be used as medicine. Either to keep your body in great condition, or it can destroy your health, thanks to massive weight gain from bad nutritional choices.

- Highly motivated people take the time to care about their health. There is no way they'd spend money ruining it.

- The best way to promote ideas and find opportunities is to always stay in touch with what's happening in the world. When you learn to do this, you'll find that you really don't have any limits.

- When you constantly analyze the trends in your own niche, you'll be able to predict dips in the market, or when something big is going to happen. Keep questioning yourself at every step.

- The moral of the story is that the world holds many solutions for us, if we care to look for them. To ignore that there are other things going on, is not only ignorant, but also short sighted. You have got to learn to grab the most from the world, as often as you can.

CHAPTER TWELVE

THE WISDOM OF SUPPORT

> *The glory of friendship is not the outstretched hand, nor the kindly smile nor the joy of companionship; it is the spiritual inspiration that comes to one when he discovers that someone else believes in him and is willing to trust him.*
>
> **– Ralph Waldo Emerson**

Personal Rewards and Why You Need Them

Working hard is a national pastime here in America – especially for business owners. There never seems to be enough time in the day, and the high-pressure circumstances take their toll on our health and social lives. One of the biggest mistakes anyone can make is working too much, or working without reward.

Everyone needs to feel like they are working for a reason! If you don't, you'll find that your batteries are impossible to recharge and you not only end up burning out, but you become de-motivated. When you work weekends, and for a disproportionate amount of money, you'll find that goals become far more difficult to achieve.

This is one of the killer reasons why so many people give up on their ideas. Like I said before, everything needs to be balanced in order to work. When you give a lot, you should be receiving a lot. When you receive, you should be giving to others. Working without paying yourself a decent salary is not on.

Have you established what you should be earning? If so, you need to make a plan to get yourself there. Once you start earning what you're worth – things will improve. You won't be so stressed out all the time, and you'll be able to make better decisions, and spot those opportunities as they arise.

The first and most crucial piece of ancient wisdom says, support yourself appropriately to build self-worth and lay the foundation for future success. When you realize that personal reward is important, you'll look for ways to lighten your load, and will adjust your work situation accordingly.

As I have explained before, if you still work on the weekend, then there's something wrong. You need time off, to spend with your loved ones – and to relax. No one can exist in a business vacuum that never ends. It will drain the life right out of you! Tempting as it is to pop into work on a Saturday, you must make plans to complete work before this, so your weekends are free. You need them.

Personal Retreats

When was the last time you had a holiday? I've always found that taking a personal retreat is fantastic for my energy levels, and gets those ideas flowing. You might have never thought of it before, but ideas come to you in the strangest of places. Most often, when you see or experience new things. That's why holidays are a great way to let loose, and let those valuable hunches come to you.

I would also encourage you to take a few books along, when you're away. Sitting down somewhere quiet, and reading inspiring literature can do wonders for the mind. My favorites are the *Bible*, *Think and Grow Rich* and Earl Nightingale's *Strangest Secret*. Read insatiably and often – remember it's all about discovering the knowledge of the world.

This can be a quarterly personal retreat, where you actively reflect on your work experiences, meditate through prayer and allow inspiration to strike. By all means take your family along. Sometimes when you're not thinking about work at all, that's when the ideas pop into your mind.

Motivation comes and goes – but like bathing, it should be done as frequently as possible! Find ways to support yourself, and your future goals. Never lose sight of the fact that your happiness and mindset will be instrumental to your success. If you mistreat yourself, or sacrifice the basics in the name of work – it will hinder your progress.

I believe that everything happens for a reason. God has given you all the tools you need to succeed, you just need to acknowledge it, set goals and plan to achieve them. We've been given the most incredible gift of logic and creation. Remember to support yourself, even through those turbulent times, when others disagree with what you are doing. Trust in God, believe in yourself – and all things are possible!

Personal and Revenue Satisfaction

You should be investing in what you want in your home, and translating that into a successful business. The greatest business leaders decide they'd like something more, then they formulate the plans to make it happen. This can be done on a small scale, as well as on a larger scale. It can also be done if you feel the need to give more, which is often the case.

Before you can run though, you must walk. Supporting yourself means realizing when your motivation is waning. A very big part of staying motivated is maintaining a positive mindset, but this often isn't enough on its own. You need rewards, and these rewards you have to give to yourself.

Don't forget to financially reward yourself, when something great has happened. Remind yourself that you've learned something valuable, and that you're so much closer to your goals because of it. You can also do this when you have tedious tasks in front of you – you know, the ones you put off doing?

Then again, there are loads of ways to keep yourself going. They don't always have to be mind-focused or financially based. Make these tasks fun. I like to reward myself after a few long hours doing something horribly boring, by hitting the gym for an hour after that. The short-term goal of reaching the gym helps me get through the work so much faster, and keeps me focused on my long-term goals.

These rewards should always fuel you. Don't get stuck in bad habits, like rewarding yourself with an hour's worth of sleep, or a large sugary snack.

At the end of the day if it doesn't contribute to your success – don't do it! Recognize the progress you're making by celebrating your little milestones.

It can be something as simple as buying a box of chocolates to share with your spouse when you get home, or going out to dinner! Personal rewards for your progress are something only you can determine. They'll enrich your learning experience, and focus you on the most important things – achieving that dream.

Take stock of how far you've come, and what you had to do to get there. Then try to figure out how much further you still need to go. You will be amazed at how fast these little personal and financial rewards will get you where you need to go!

Capitalism and Global Freedom

This section has no ulterior motive, or party to push, or ax to grind. But I feel it must be said. Capital on its own, in our day and age, is the most underestimated and misunderstood weapon for success that exists in America. Yet it's a gift that gives to American's whether they realize it or not.

Capital, means the highly motivated, organized men who focus on planning and inventing with the use of money, for the best possible practical applications - to benefit all mankind. These pioneers are inventors, physicians, businessmen, marketing gurus, chemists, and engineers, who are highly specialized by comparison in their given fields.

They support the arts, colleges and universities, hospitals, and the majority of the cost of government. In summary, Capitalists are the 'brains' of our civilization - as it is from their creation and efforts that the fabric of society finds itself woven. Money without the use of intellect, is dangerous. When properly used through planning, it is of essential importance to all mankind.

We don't flex this muscle as a people, (in my humble opinion) like we used to, and for that, it has become weak. The men that do flex this muscle are perceived as being extremely tall, and in the absence of leadership, become ultra wealthy. Think about this – in times past, when a route across America was discovered to become extremely more efficient to have a railroad, than a wagon, those railroads didn't spring up from the ground.

A 2000 page bill wasn't passed in Congress to fund it. The railroad was formed by a call to civilization to organize labor, and from the ability of great men to employ imagination, desire, faith, and persistence. These men are known as capitalists. They are defined by their desire to achieve, invent, construct, and to earn the riches that can be attained, by laying a pathway of such large services in place for many men after them, to walk, after they are gone.

Making Money?

Our culture today is too obsessed with 'making' money. You can't 'make' money. The only people who 'make' money, actually print it, and they work in a mint. Money can only be earned, and ancient wisdom says that you can only receive a certain level of financial gain - to the level of that which you give.

Historically speaking, I believe we are seeing more of a transfer of these great creative opportunities being pulled away from men, and gathered at municipal and government levels to execute on. The greatest danger isn't the jobs that may never happen, but that mankind is being lulled away from their purpose, from pushing their imagination, and creating at their highest possible levels.

Man is being lulled to sleep, being trained that you are entitled to a good 'job' so that you can 'make' a good living, and it is absolutely crippling the dreams and desires of what men can truly become. Creativity will, I believe, be stifled more and more. It's not that it will be impossible to succeed, it's just not encouraged as much as it was before.

Capitalism in Context

I want everyone to be great, but in a climate where we are trained to 'just do a job' and not create one, we are living in a time when the absence of the climate itself, is a sufficient discouragement for men to never ascend to leadership. We have allowed people in suits to actually 'convince us' that we are not good enough to do it, and that we need help.

If they get to choose, then that means you get to pay for it, and it's a power play that should be in YOUR hands. The decision to be big and collaborate should be undertaken by your ingenuity, not someone else saying, just pay us, 'We got this!' Power mongering has denigrated the creative efforts in America. We are training our kids that being a leader, a creator, in this fashion is wrong, or something to be despised.

For more than 100 years, radicals, dishonest politicians, and labor leaders refer to this as 'predatory interest' or 'Wall Street.' The playbook hasn't changed, yet the volume of media that we are given and now with public education backing the message, our kids are transferred into the enlistment of the streets, or jobs, and are not 'creating,' because who wants to be a 'pig', 'thief', or corruptor?

Leadership isn't leadership in America anymore. Men in power are pandering to the absolute worst behaviors in man, just to get a vote, and we in mass are perfectly okay, why? Because the pathway to true success has been covered over, it's been hidden under cover of nonsense, and propaganda.

It's to the detriment of the creation that we don't have, to the people who are living as drones, and aren't awake, alive and living their dreams and supporting dreams in others. We are developing small men, if men at all.

Pick Your Poison

I also want to separate capitalists from criminals. Criminals themselves do not espouse to true capitalism. Again, capitalism says, you can have in relation to what you give. A true capitalist is actually a VERY high-level servant at the core. Criminals espouse to something for nothing; they try to avoid the ancient wisdom by "Sowing nothing, and then hoping to reap something big."

The fact that the common headlines are adopted by radicals, dishonest politicians, and again the labor leaders, that capitalism is poisonous - is unconscionable to me.

Criminals who cloak themselves as capitalists are pure evil. If we define a person who creates, organizes labor smartly, for the good and service of all, can we really call someone who comes on the scene and swindles a bunch of people, a capitalist?

Don't we have politicians, who under the guise of public service, arrive in Congress, assist their friends with hefty government contracts and their own financial interest, and just a few years after leaving office, are far more rich than when they came to office (in public service!), and yet, do we call ALL politicians 'Political Pigs?'

There are criminals who sneak into any venue, under the guise of being like everyone else, and they are called a fraud. There are criminals that become heads of organizations that don't treat their employees well. There are politicians that will reward horrendous behavior and baseless ideas to the overall detriment of our people. Behind all of this, it is important to know that opportunity is boundless, and possibly wider than ever.

Never be distracted by any appraisal of how much money or opportunity you think exists in the world – it is there and it's everywhere. We spend billions of dollars on the most minor things in America. Each year we spend 7 billion dollars on chocolate, 38 billion on hair care products, 2.3 billion on deodorant and 18 billion on coffee.

You only need to drop your services directly in front of demand, and you will see success. The table is set with opportunity. It is everywhere. America gives everyone opportunity to develop useful services, and to collect riches in proportion to those services rendered. The truth about opportunity is that the 'view' of the opportunity is what is most important.

If business, in your head, is good, then you will see opportunity. If business is bad and perceived that way in the mind, then that is what you will have in life.

The system does not and cannot 'see' your color, your educational background, your looks, it only values what you give, and in return, feeds back the reward in proportion to those services that you've offered. The system DOES NOT promise something for nothing, and shame on the country for 'corporately' producing such a wide safety net.

Our society - and specifically - many cities have completely collapsed under this treatment of people. As Napoleon Hill so eloquently put in the early 20th century: *"The system cannot promise something for nothing because the system itself is controlled by the law of economics which neither recognizes nor tolerates for long, getting without giving."*

Your Group Power Breakfast

Now that you understand supporting yourself in context, despite the system that is against you – it might be clear that help is in order. Remember iron on iron? You need to build up a network of motivated friends. These friends will help to push you forward, instead of holding you back.

Ideally, these personalities will understand your ideas, and may even help improve them with conversation. These iron friends are extremely competitive, inspirational people that would like nothing more than to see you succeed. They hold you to higher standards than other people, and will be harder on you during your pursuit for success and achievement.

You should host group power breakfasts fairly often, where these extraordinary friends meet and discuss plans with each other. This powerful group will be your keystone, and will support you where others fail. You'll need this group to help you along your path. There's a great saying I'm always reminded of whenever I host group power breakfasts.

Great minds talk about ideas, average minds talk about events and weak minds talk about people. In your pursuit to be great, and to give back to the world through innovation and creation – these friends are invaluable. You can take turns hosting the event at different places, or at the homes of your group members.

Just like they are there to help you along your path, so you should be there to listen to their plans – and urge them forward. The more you give of your time to these iron friends, the better their plans will turn out. It's your duty to help them be successful, just as much as it's their duty to inspire you, to become more than you are now.

Get that group power breakfast going. It's done in the morning, so that you can feed off that competitive energy all day long. It's best to do it on a weekday as well. That way, you can charge into work and crush it, right after you've been inspired! If none of your iron friends have ever done anything like it before – explain the concept. They'll only be too willing to join, because it will help them too! Something as simple as incorporating a group power breakfast into your month, can change the way you act on ideas. Suddenly you're accountable, and all eyes are watching. Use this to your advantage.

The Amplification of Business Success

To amplify your success in business, improve your support systems. Review these great tips to stay in touch with your goals.

- Everyone needs to feel like they are working for a reason! If you don't, you'll find that your batteries are impossible to recharge and you not only end up burning out, but you become de-motivated.

- The first and most crucial piece of ancient wisdom says, support yourself appropriately to build self worth and lay the foundation for future success. When you realize that personal reward is important, you'll look for ways to lighten your load, and will adjust your work situation accordingly.

- Take a personal retreat, it's fantastic for your energy levels, and gets those ideas flowing. Bring some inspiring books along!

- Motivation comes and goes – but like bathing, it should be done as frequently as possible! Find ways to support yourself, and your future goals. Never lose sight of the fact that your happiness and mindset will be instrumental to your success.

- Don't get stuck in bad habits, like rewarding yourself with an hour's worth of sleep, or a large sugary snack. At the end of the day if it doesn't contribute to your success – don't do it!

- Money without the use of intellect, is dangerous. When properly used through planning, it is of essential importance to all mankind.

- You can't 'make' money. The only people who 'make' money, actually print it, and they work in a mint. Money can only be earned, and ancient wisdom says that you can only receive a certain level of financial gain - to the level of that which you give.

- Politicians shadow your advancement by making you think that, you becoming someone great, is somehow 'poisonous' by virtue of capitalism.

- A true capitalist is actually a VERY high-level servant at the core.

- "The system cannot promise something for nothing, because the system itself is controlled by the law of economics, which neither recognizes nor tolerates for long, getting without giving."

- You should host group power breakfasts fairly often, where these extraordinary friends meet and discuss plans with each other. This powerful group will be your keystone, and will support you where others fail.

- Something as simple as incorporating a group power breakfast into your month, can change the way you act on ideas. Suddenly you're accountable, and all eyes are watching.

CHAPTER THIRTEEN

THE WISDOM OF SPIRITUAL POWER

> *It is extraordinary power from God, not talent, that wins the day. It is extraordinary spiritual unction not extraordinary mental power, that we need. Mental power may fill a chapel but spiritual power fills the church with soul anguish. Mental power may gather a large congregation. but only spiritual power will save souls. What we need is spiritual power.*
>
> **– Charles. H. Spurgeon**

Living a Spiritual Life

In this book, we discussed many different areas of life and the most important pieces of ancient wisdom that can be employed to bring massive change and improvement in life. Of all of the different pieces of wisdom and insight that I have been fortunate to gain, none is more powerful than or remotely as important as what I will share with you now.

The catalyst of true joy, happiness and success stems from this one single principle of spiritual life. Its discovery changed me beyond what any seminar presenter, PH.D, efficiency coach or guru could ever hope to add to my life. In fact, if I spent the rest of my life with them each and every single day, it wouldn't come close to helping as much as this single piece of principle.

When we desire to grow in any facet of our lives, our core blueprint generally helps or causes us more challenges in ways unique to each of us. As an example, some people are MUCH more athletically gifted than others. These folks can run faster, adapt to sports more easily and metabolize food like no one else! They can eat bags of cookies, and you wouldn't notice, but someone without this blueprint may struggle to adapt to a new sport, and eating an extra French fry could, for them, tip the scale up a few notches over night!

The blueprint of an intellectually strong person would allow them to be considerably more gifted than others. There are people who can read entire books in 20 or 30 minutes, with retention, where the mass majority, it could take six to eight hours to learn that same material. Testing for this group is a breeze.

Much like many of the other principles of wisdom in this book, the principle itself is a universally immutable law, meaning it is as basic as cause and effect. You can be as dependent on the response from an application as you can that a dish dropped on the hard floor will crash into pieces.

In the application of spiritual power, you will learn in this chapter that gaining spiritual life is not contingent in any way on any one person's physical or mental capacities. In fact, in comparison of all of the other items in this book, this transition is the easiest to apply as it does not discriminate on any given factors or attributes in you.

Given the marvelous nature of us as humans and the overwhelming uniqueness in all of us being more of a headline in the defining of us each as people, in regards to our "spiritual condition", we are by comparison more "equal" as humans than by almost any other aspect that can be measured.

We have talked in-depth about ancient wisdom and the

modern application of those principles to bring success, but have you ever stopped to think how much money it would take to make a person's life perfect? True happiness in and of itself is the satisfaction of knowing that you are continually fulfilling your core purpose, the reason you are here – the essence of spiritual power.

Obviously, you know through my own reference points for success that the Bible is my choice of authority for wisdom, for understanding faith, and for finding quality in life. Whether aware of it or not, many people live by Biblical principles; they apply universal laws and experience resulting success regardless of their knowledge of the source of this wisdom.

I want to take this a step further – the Bible is not just a practical book to manage our success, but the Bible is the singular authority on the spiritual condition of man. Man did not write or create this book, but instead wrote under inspiration of the Spirit of God, kind of like a secretary writing a letter dictated by the boss.

Like many other things that we discussed in this book, to be powerful, successful and focused, you must take inventory. You have to be intellectually honest with yourself. If I were sitting with you right now, as friends, we might start the discussion by saying

What do you believe spiritually? Do you have any kind of spiritual beliefs?

You might answer this in a number of ways. You might say, "I have a family member who is a preacher," or "I grew up in a certain faith," or something of the sort. But think about that. What do you believe spiritually? If we were speaking right now completely casually and DEFINITELY as friends, what would you see us discussing at that point?

In prompting our discussion of the pursuit of spiritual power and assuming we didn't discuss this already when we discussed our spiritual beliefs, I would ask, "To you, who is Jesus Christ?" Have you ever pondered this question before? Do you have an answer in your own mind now? The answers to this question would often range from some saying "He was a great teacher, or even a great prophet," to those that have spiritual power referring to Jesus Christ in the personal sense, such as, "my savior" or "my friend".

My next question might warrant a simple yes or no. Do you believe in heaven or hell? Regardless how or where our discussion of heaven or hell might have gone and whether or not you share that you believe in the two places, my next question would be, "If you were to die today where would you go?"

My final question as we discuss the application of spiritual power as friends would be this: "If what you believe was not true, would you want to know?" Assuming the answer is that you would want to know, you have extended me permission to share with you one of the greatest changes that I've ever personally allowed into my life.

One thing we all share, no matter who we are, where we come from, or our abilities or lack thereof, we are all born with some common characteristics.

The first one is that we are not perfect! In fact, thousands of years ago, the Bible told us in Romans 3:23, "All of us have sinned and fall short of the glory of God". No matter how hard we try, perfection has not, nor ever will be attained. God has this "glory" but we do not. I know when you married your spouse, you felt that you could possibly argue this, but it's true! We have all done something we wish we could take back. "All have sinned" – that's us!

Another important fact to understand is that the "wages of our sin cause separation" from this perfect God. The scripture in Romans 6:23 actually says, "For the wages of sin is death".

We as human beings know that our bad must somehow be in a balance with our good. We think of our good like this. "I was baptized as a child; that should help me out on some of these 'sins'." "I served in a local soup kitchen to help feed the homeless; that was pretty good, and should count for something in the end, right?" Unfortunately, our sin is so harmful that the scripture writes it as a prescription for death. We could toil doing good, but that doesn't change the 'price' that we owe for our sin, death. How could one be perfect enough to reverse that kind of price? But fortunately it doesn't end with that statement! Romans 6:23 in its entirety says "For the wages of sin is death, but the gift of God is eternal life in Jesus Christ our Lord". That verse continues with an amazing promise that regardless of the heavy cost of our sin, that God has offered LIFE through His Son, Jesus.

Notice one very important thing that this verse tells us - that the wages of 'SIN' are death; there is no 's' after the word sin, making it clear that the wage of one wrong deed merits me eternal separation from God.

Another final point to take away is that you gain life by coming into a relationship with Jesus, and it really does not have anything to do with religion. We have ritualized this in so many ways, and in many cases lost this simple, basic truth!

What about this Jesus and what is so special that He could offer me anything? In John 14:6, Jesus gives us one of his clearest explanations "I am the way and the truth and the life. No one comes to the father except through me." Jesus is very clear on one thing in this verse - that there is no other way to God (the Father) except through him. This is important to understand.

In life, we have choices everywhere. We can change our eye color or hair color; we can buy a new car every year if we can handle the payment, and we can even get a complete facelift, but the word of God tells us that in a world full of choices, that there is one access to God. Understand, that God too is a gentleman, you don't have to "choose" Him if you do not want to, but that doesn't change the fact, that there is one result of sin, which is death. Jesus, God's Son, offers us life if we chose it, but the fact remains that the choice was never forced on us and that it is up to each of us.

When looking at these words in the Bible, I reflect on my own life that when I reconciled all of these things with me, I was seven years old. Even at a young age, it was so simple. I'm a pretty simple person, and honestly, I am grateful for a God who knows that someone like me needed such an easy access to spiritual life so that I could experience His power in my life!

Romans 10:9-11 tells us, "That if you confess with your mouth 'Jesus is Lord', and believe in your heart that God raised him from the dead, you will be saved. For it is with your heart that you believe and are justified, and it is with your mouth that you confess and are saved." As the Scripture says, "Everyone who trusts in Him will never be put to shame".

These verses are hard to grasp, but you really can have your sins forgiven by a loving God. It's hard to believe, as you read this verse again, you may have something horrible in your mind such as a person you stole from or someone you may have hurt through adultery, alcoholism, hatred towards a spouse or co-worker.

Do you think this verse too good to be true!? Read this verse five times if you have to, and understand, that whatever it is, your sins can be forgiven. The day Jesus died, he was hanging from a cross with nails through his hands and feet, and there were crosses on either side of him and on each a criminal hung to die. One criminal mocked Jesus, and the other, accepted him as God's son saying, "Jesus, remember me when you come into your kingdom". Like these criminals, sin sentences us to death, and we are offered a choice. Some will mock, and some will accept.

2 Corinthians 5:15, the Bible reads, "And He died for all, that those who live should no longer live for themselves but for Him who died for them and was raised again."

Spiritual power means that you are surrendering your life to Jesus as Savior, that we are no longer slaves to whatever symptoms of sin that have for so long strangled the joy from our lives. Spiritual power through surrender to Jesus Christ brings an inner transformation to have new life!

"Here I am! I stand at the door and knock. If anyone hears my voice and opens the door, I will come in and eat with him, and he with me." Revelations 3:20.

Friend, I am not here to convince you of anything. I am not knocking, I am not selling, but I am sharing my life with you, as I have done from Chapter One of this book. It is Jesus who can tempt your heart, not me.

My friend, if there is any message to be learned in this chapter, it is this - take it seriously, more than anything that can be said in this book, or any other. No other message matters more in your entire life than this message. If you ask Jesus to come into your life, He will. Notice the Scripture doesn't say, Jesus is going to open the door and come in, all He does is knock. The opening of that door is your choice.

Are you a sinner?

Do you want forgiveness of sins?

Do you believe Jesus died on the cross for you and rose again?

Are you willing to surrender your life to Jesus Christ?

Are you ready to invite Jesus into your heart and into your life?

If you agree, pray this simple prayer to the Lord, right where you are.

"Lord Jesus, I know that I am a sinner. I know that you are God, and that you died to pay for my sin. I believe that you rose from the dead, proving that you are God. Right now, in the best way I know how, I ask you to be my Lord, my Savior and my God. Thank you, Jesus, for dying for me. Help me now to live for you. Amen."

If you did pray this prayer for the very first time, please email me (info@wisehorizon.com) and let me know that! I assure you that I will personally review this email and will not share it with anyone without your permission, but I want to celebrate your new life with you and do want to be a crucial support for you in this new decision. I have some information that I would like to email you, if you would send me that note.

The Amplification of Spiritual Power

- We are all coequals on a journey and we all share the common thread that we are imperfect.

- Our shared symptom of imperfection puts us squarely in need of a Savior, and spiritual life is granted through a relationship with Jesus Christ.

- The catalyst of true joy, happiness and success stems from this one single principle of spiritual life.

- True happiness in and of itself is the satisfaction of knowing that you are continually fulfilling your core purpose, the reason you are here – the essence of spiritual power.

- Jesus, God's Son, offers us life if we choose it, but the fact remains that the choice was never forced on us and that it is up to each of us.

- Spiritual power through surrender to Jesus Christ brings an inner transformation to have new life!

- Prayer is a powerful motivator

CONCLUSION

We've reached the end of Ancient Secrets, and the beginning of your new life as an innovative achiever. Every single one of these ancient secrets I've applied in my own life. They work. It's just a matter of building the motivation and momentum to see your goals come to fruition.

Now, I want you to go into the world and make a difference. Be who you were always meant to be – a creator.

Ancient wisdom tells us that you must develop these core traits in order to be successful –

- Be focused on your goals

- Use your burning desire to make them a reality

- Have faith that your desires will come true

- Maintain a positive mindset and learn to control your thoughts

- Learn to give, and you will receive ten fold

- Teach yourself self discipline and do what needs to be done

- Think and dream big using your powerful imagination

- Become an innovator and create

- Cast your mind into the future and plan to get there

- Always put your happiness first

- Prepare your mind and body for success

- Learn to support yourself, and benefit from the support of others

I cannot think of a better way to end my book than with the main points from the powerful speech delivered by Steve Jobs, the greatest innovator of our time.

In it, he tells three stories.

The First Story Is About Connecting The Dots.

Steve was adopted, on condition that his new parents went to college, and would send him one day. Later it was discovered they didn't go to college, but they promised to send him – to give him a better chance in life.

He went to a very expensive college, but found little value in it. College, didn't help him find his calling. Instead, he was spending large amounts of his adoptive parent's money, for nothing. So, Steve dropped out. He left the boring classes behind him, and attended classes that interested him as an alternative.

Later in life, he discovered that following his intuition and curiosity was priceless. The Calligraphy class he attended had no application in the 'real' world, but it became the inspiration for the Mac typography, ten years later. If he hadn't attended that class, it's likely that all computers would have uniform typefaces. *"... You can't connect the dots looking forward; you can only connect them looking backwards. So, you have to trust that the dots will somehow connect in your future. You have to trust in something — your gut, destiny, life, karma, whatever. This approach has never let me down, and it has made all the difference in my life."*

The Second Story Is About Love And Loss.

From a garage company, Apple grew into a company worth 2 billion dollars, with over 4000 employees. Then Steve got fired.

There was a clash of future vision, and the Board of Directors voted him out. It was devastating.

Many months later, he started over. In the end, getting fired was the best thing that ever happened to him, and heightened his creativity. He started a company called NeXT, and Pixar as well. Pixar became the first company in the world to produce a full 3D length film – Toy Story. Then Apple bought NeXT, and suddenly he was back there. He also met and married the love of his life, Laurene.

"Sometimes life hits you in the head with a brick. Don't lose faith. I'm convinced that the only thing that kept me going was that I loved what I did. You've got to find what you love. And that is as true for your work as it is for your lovers."

"And the only way to do great work is to love what you do. If you haven't found it yet, keep looking. Don't settle. As with all matters of the heart, you'll know when you find it. And, like any great relationship, it just gets better and better as the years roll on. So keep looking until you find it. Don't settle."

The Third Story Is About Death.

"If you live each day as if it was your last, someday you'll most certainly be right." Using mortality as his guidepost, Steve set rules as to what he should and shouldn't be doing with his life. When death is involved, it strips away the chaff, and leaves the important things behind.

Steve was then diagnosed with Cancer, and told he had a few months to live. Later that day, they discovered it was a rare form of Cancer, curable by surgery. The near death experience, Steve said, is likely the single best invention of life. Time is limited, so don't be trapped by what everyone else thinks or does.

"Don't let the noise of others' opinions drown out your own inner voice. And most important, have the courage to follow your heart and intuition. They somehow already know what you truly want to become. Everything else is secondary."
Steve Jobs, (1955-2011)

God created all of us with the power to be extraordinary. You have the ability, and now you have the tool to use to unlock that drive within yourself.

Right now, you're at crossroads.

Do you accept this ancient knowledge and apply it in your life, or do you close this book and return to mediocrity, and a life unfulfilled?

This is your chance! Don't let it pass you by.

Carpe Diem my friends!

- Jared W Jones

www.wisehorizon.com

REFERENCES

Latumahina, Donald. *How to focus, five levels of mental focus you might not be aware of*, Life Optimizer, http://www.lifeoptimizer.org/2008/05/14/how-to-focus-five-levels-of-mental-focus-you-might-not-aware-of/

Humbert, Philip E (2003) *Top 10 Secrets of Getting Rich*, http://www.successconsciousness.com/guest_articles/secrets_getting_rich.htm

Hill, Napoleon, *Chapter 2 Desire: The turning point of all achievement*, Think and Grow Rich, http://soilandhealth.org/03sov/0304spiritpsych/030413.Hill.Think.and.Grow.Rich.pdf

Kotelnikov, Vadim, *Charles Schwab: From a Small Firm to the World's Leader,* http://www.1000ventures.com/business_guide/cs_fast_company_schwab.html

----

Sasson, Remez, *Positive Thinking Your Key to Success,* Success Consciousness, http://www.successconsciousness.com/index_00003a.htm

Positive thinking techniques to build self esteem (2011) http://www.silvalifesystem.com/articles/positive-thinking/positive-thinking-techniques/

Thought Awareness, Rational Thinking, and Positive Thinking, http://www.mindtools.com/pages/article/newTCS_06.htm

Positive Thinking, http://www.guideposts.org/positive-thinking

----

Bilanich, Bud (13 April 2010) *An Abundance Mentality Leads to Success,* http://www.budbilanich.com/competence/an-abundance-mentality-leads-to-success/

Owens, Harry, ABUNDANCE VERSUS SCARCITY MENTALITY, St. Charles Medical Center, http://www.healinghealthcareassoc.org/documents/abundance-vs-scarcity.pdf

Deffinbaugh, Bob (study) *The Parable of the Talents* (Matthew 25:14-30; Luke 19:12-28) http://bible.org/seriespage/parable-talents-matthew-2514-30-luke-1912-28

Middleton, Robert (26 May 2008) *Passive or Proactive Marketing?* http://actionplan.blogs.com/weblog/2008/05/passive-or-proactive-marketing.html

Harrison, Mark, *10 Positive Habits to Cultivate*, http://www.thechangeblog.com/positive-habits-to-cultivate/

Trent, (9 April 2009) *Establishing Positive Habits and Routines*, http://www.thesimpledollar.com/2009/04/09/establishing-positive-habits-and-routines/

Newby-Clark, Ian, *Three Effective Ways to Enhance Your Willpower*, http://zenhabits.net/three-effective-ways-to-enhance-your-willpower/

Parker-Pope, Tara, (6 December 2007) *How to Boost Your Willpower*, http://well.blogs.nytimes.com/2007/12/06/how-to-boost-your-willpower/

Pavlina, Steve (7 June 2005) *Self-Discipline: Willpower*, http://www.stevepavlina.com/blog/2005/06/self-discipline-willpower/

Why Imagination Is Important In Business, http://www.geekbusiness.com/2011/03/why-imagination-is-important-in-business/

Creativity, Imagination and Your Business, (6 January 2011) http://www.abilitysuccessgrowth.com/2011/01/creativity-imagination-and-your-business/

How to use imagination to extend your business in a creative and innovative way, http://www.uniquemarketingtool.com/how-to-use-imagination-to-extend-your-business-in-a-creative-and-innovative-way/

Tim Berners-Lee, http://www.w3.org/People/Berners-Lee/

Ralph Baer, http://www.pong-story.com/rhbaer.htm

John Logie Baird (1888 – 1946) http://www.bbc.co.uk/history/historic_figures/baird_logie.shtml

Steve Jobs, http://allaboutstevejobs.com/bio/bio.html

Bell's Telephone, http://fi.edu/franklin/inventor/bell.html

Beals, Gerald (1996) *Thomas Alva Edison,* http://www.thomasedison.com/Inventions.htm

7 Habits of Highly Innovative People, http://thinksimplenow.com/creativity/7-habits-of-highly-innovative-people/

Spradlin, Alexander, *The Empathic Misanthrope,* http://www.psychologytoday.com/blog/the-empathic-misanthrope/201109/fake-it-til-you-make-it

Plevin, Julia (December 2011) Startup and the city: Fake it until you make it, http://venturebeat.com/2011/12/09/startup-and-the-city-fake-it-until-you-make-it/

Understanding Human Happiness and Well-Being, http://www.sustainablescale.org/attractivesolutions/understandinghumanhappinessandwellbeing.aspx

Veenhoven, Ruut, *ADVANCES IN UNDERSTANDING HAPPINESS,* Published in French in Revue Québécoise de Psychologie, 1997, vol 18, pp 29-7, http://repub.eur.nl/res/pub/16324/97c-full.pdf

Happiness In America: An Old Parable, (2008) http://www.
screamtobegreen.com/2008/01/happiness-in-america-an-old-
parable/

Pychyl, Timothy A (13 February 2009) *Fear of Failure,* The latest
research on fear of failure and procrastination, http://www.
psychologytoday.com/blog/dont-delay/200902/fear-failure

7 Ways to Overcome the Fear of Failure, http://www.pickthebrain.
com/blog/overcome-fear-of-failure/

Gruenemay, Jennifer, (17 January 2011) *Rise and Shine: Top 5 Morning
Exercise Benefits* http://www.lifescript.com/Body/Shape/Workout/
Rise_and_Shine_Top_5_Morning_Exercise_Benefits.aspx

Dr. Mercola (4 January 2011) *Why Exercising at This Time of Day
is FAR Better than Any Other Time,* http://fitness.mercola.com/
sites/fitness/archive/2011/01/04/the-benefits-of-exercising-before-
breakfast.aspx

Finklestein, Ron, *Why is a company culture so important?* http://
www.evancarmichael.com/Business-Coach/188/Why-is-a-
company-culture-so-important.html

Why Podcast? http://www.podtopia.net/articles/whypodcast.shtml

Watlington, Amanda G. (26 October 2006) *What Is Podcasting
and Why Bother?* http://www.wilsonweb.com/newmedia/
watlington-why-podcasting.htm

Jobs, Steve, Stanford Report, June 14, 2005, http://news.
stanford.edu/news/2005/june15/jobs-061505.html

www.ingramcontent.com/pod-product-compliance
Lightning Source LLC
Chambersburg PA
CBHW021053090426
42738CB00006B/323